MAX LINDER
Father of Film Comedy

By
SNORRE SMÁRI MATHIESEN

MAX LINDER: Father of Film Comedy
By SNORRE SMÁRI MATHIESEN
© 2018 SNORRE SMÁRI MATHIESEN. ALL RIGHTS RESERVED.
No part of this book may be reproduced in any form or by any means, electronic, mechanical, digital, photocopying, or recording, except for inclusion of a review, without permission in writing from the publisher or Author.

Published in the USA by:
BearManor Media
1317 Edgewater Dr #110
Orlando, FL 32804
www.bearmanormedia.com

Perfect ISBN: 978-1-62933-207-9
Case ISBN: 978-1-62933-208-6
BearManor Media, Orlando, Florida
Printed in the United States of America
Book design by Robbie Adkins, www.adkinsconsult.com

TABLE OF CONTENTS

Acknowledgments... v
Introduction vi
Chapter 1 Max Toots His Roots 1
Chapter 2 Max Engaged on Stage 4
Chapter 3 Max the Career Pioneer................................ 10
Chapter 4 Max's Surefire Attire 17
Chapter 5 Max Exceeds Deed 20
Chapter 6 Max Stacks Up.. 25
Chapter 7 Max's Murky Malady....................................31
Chapter 8 Max on Track 34
Chapter 9 Max Makes Director................................... 39
Chapter 10 Max Back in the Sack................................ 46
Chapter 11 Max Mixes with the Masses........................... 52
Chapter 12 Max Matures on Tours 60
Chapter 13 Max and War Furor................................... 73
Photo Gallery.. 82
Chapter 14 Max Operates in the States 103
Chapter 15 Max's Reign Wanes 118
Chapter 16 Max's Keen Return to the Screen 123
Chapter 17 Max Scored with a Sword 126
Chapter 18 Max Vaunts with Gance.............................. 136
Chapter 19 Max Pix Clicks 143
Chapter 20 Max Descends to His End 149
Chapter 21 Max's Intestacy Legacy............................. 153
Chapter 22 Max Enshrined in Time 159
Filmography 163
Bibliography 176
Chapter Notes... 179

ACKNOWLEDGEMENTS

This book owes an incalculable debt to Mr. Georg Renken, the prime Max Linder expert from Germany, who generously provided me access to material available on his website www.max-linder.de, (which any fan of Linder is obliged to visit), including a vast collection of newspaper articles, as well as his painstaking filmography and incredible survey on Linder's stage appearances between 1904-1908. Renken's "Chronicle" on Linder's life was also very helpful. In addition, his expertise came to supreme use while I dealt with a court case (and jewel theft) in which Linder was involved in 1913, as Renken clarified the largely conflicting reports of this incident (see Chapter 12). He also came to the rescue while I wrote about an accident that Linder suffered around Christmas 1922, specifying the time and place of the mishap (see Chapter 18). I cannot thank Renken enough for all of this.

Many thanks also to Bibliothèque Nationale de France, The Norwegian National Library, Elephind.com, as well as *The New York Times*, *Aftenposten*, and *Dagens Nyheter*, for their respective digitalized archives of old newspapers and various journals that have also been most useful as source material. Mr. Henri Bousquet's own careful filmography of early Pathé releases—including Linder's—also became very handy.

I am grateful to Mrs. Lisa Stein Haven, who thoroughly encouraged this project while writing an upcoming book on Linder of her own.

Thank you to BearManor Media, including Ben Ohmart and my editor David Menefee, for their belief in this project.

Finally, a bountiful thanks to Mrs. Maud Linder, who kindly responded to my letters with questions in 2006-2007, and whose tireless work to preserve the legacy of her father has proved invaluable to a generation of silent film fans.

INTRODUCTION

"Max Linder was the first international movie star, equally popular in Moscow as in Buenos Aires, in Paris as in New York."

Such read the caption beneath a handsome publicity photo of Max, taken at the height of his worldwide fame, in Rune Walderkranz's Swedish book on film history, *Filmens Historia: De första hundra åren - Del 1, Pionjärtiden 1880-1920*.* I had been browsing through this huge brick of a book for several minutes and was just about to leave the rather cramped, used bookstore in central Oslo, having resisted the itch to spend all loose change thus far. The shot of Max in top hat, accompanied by Walderkranz's brief but eloquent summary of his career, had me enamored—and I wound up emptying that week's pocket money after all. It was January 2005; I was in my teens.

Although much too young to have had opportunity to absorb old-time flickers as much as a film historian would likely deem obligatory, I'd been a diehard fan of silent comedy for several years even at that point in life, my fascination triggered when I first watched, and fell in love with, Charlie Chaplin's *Modern Times* at eight. I soon developed a keen interest in other films of the era, as well as the era itself. With YouTube being still some years ahead in the future while I grew up, my local video store happily maintained a healthy supply of Chaplin and Buster Keaton on tape, as well as some of the fabulously hilarious Laurel & Hardy two-reelers (in sound, granted). What's more, they also provided a couple of Robert Youngson's silent comedy cavalcades, *The Golden Age of Comedy* (1957) and *When Comedy Was King* (1960)—thus ensuring my introduction to more forgotten stars, such as Harry Langdon, Roscoe Arbuckle, Mabel Normand, Ben Turpin, Snub Pollard, Billy Bevan, Will Rogers, and Charley Chase. Throughout my adolescence, I found these mirth-makers to make life jollier in a way that few contemporary comedians did; they aided me through some good and some less good times.

* Translates "Film History: The First Hundred Years, Part 1 - The Pioneers, 1880-1920."

It was Rune Walderkranz's massive book that made me aware of Max Linder. Virtually none of his films had been available to me at the time, save for a few seconds of the short film, *Vive la vie de garçon* (*Troubles of a Grass Widower*, 1908), in an obscure Chaplin-documentary. I immediately wanted to know more about this stylish comedian, but was frustrated to discover that relatively little had been written about him in English (although in retrospect, I wondered if this didn't make him all the more compelling). I sought out all films of his that I could possibly find.

The absence of a book-length biography on Max Linder in English has struck me as rather curious in later years. This is an age, after all, where "every" major or semi-major comedian of the silent film era appears to be granted a book-length study in due order—ranging from Ford Sterling to Lloyd Hamilton. There was a time once when only the greatest icons were considered worthy of thorough examinations, such as Chaplin, Keaton, Harold Lloyd, and barely Langdon and Arbuckle, but this has thankfully changed for the better in the last two decades or so.

Yet the attempts to compress Linder's life story into book form have been few and far between. In fairness, there do exist a couple of books in French, most notably his daughter Maud's dazzling-looking biography in coffee-table format, *Les Dieux Du Cinéma Muet Max Linder* (1992), and one study that Charles Ford did in the 1960s. Maud has also written an autobiography, *Max Linder était mon pere*, which inevitably provides information on her father, as well. (I was about half-way through with this book's manuscript when I learned that Lisa Stein Haven, author of several superb Chaplin books, was working on a book on Max Linder in English, but this has not yet become available as of this writing.)

It may seem only natural that the assortment in French is slightly superior, since Linder himself was a native of France and did by far most of his work there. Be that as it may, Linder differs from his French contemporaries—André Deed, Charles "Prince" Seigneur—in that he, to this day, is regularly mentioned in the same breath as Hollywood giants such as Chaplin and Keaton. One may partly explain this with the fact that Max did star in at least six American films, but, more importantly, his total body of work has simply aged better than that of any other film comedian prior to Chaplin's debut in 1914. Confidently sporting upscale tuxedo and black top hat, Max's graceful silhouette resembled an actual human being—a real gentleman—despite a frequent penchant for infantile impulses. He was, in the words of Rune Walderkranz, "the first [character] in film history to be portrayed with psychological credibility and, amidst all the situational comedy, a certain finesse."[1]

Unlike the cases of Chaplin or Keaton, the prospect of scrutinizing Max's body of work remains limited at best, since most of his hundreds of films are lost. I will provide personal reviews of a selection of individual titles, along with contemporary press reviews, preferably not just from France or the United States, but also several more European countries, including, when possible, my home country, Norway. With this I hope to illustrate the degree of Max's international fame during his lifetime. (I will not cover every single film he made, or even all of his films that I have been able to view myself.) Beware that I will also provide some information on film history, which to some may appear redundant, as I wish to make the book user-friendly to readers not too familiar with early films. (A few things should be evident to all readers, such as the fact that motion pictures initially and for several decades were silent.)

The chapters on Max's final years and aftermath may strike some as uncomfortable reading. I frankly found it emotionally challenging to write the latter parts of this book, so bleak did the comedian's later life become. I have wished not to glorify the man behind the charming "Max," but instead try to sustain a balanced mindset as far as possible. I set out to write this book most of all to celebrate his genius as a major pioneer of film comedy, which is why I became interested in his life in the first place.

I am happy to say that, since my own discovery of Max in 2005, quite a bit more has been written on him in English, in the form of blog posts on the Web, etc. A *definitive* biography on the comedian will no doubt hit the bookshelves one day. In fact, I am confident that Lisa Stein Haven's upcoming biography will prove to be such a book. This is, however, an attempt to provide readers with a decent overview on his life and career. I do hope it may be useful to fans of the great comedian, and possibly inspire the unfamiliar to seek out his films, just as Rune Walderkranz's book once did to me.

-Snorre Smári Mathiesen, May 2017

(Spring 2023, Update: After writing this book in 2017, I discovered some things I was dissatisfied with. A few times, when describing certain plots in Linder's films, I adopted a rather "ironic" tone which I now think was unnecessary. There are some other things in the book which I think I could've phrased better, as well. Also, I've found a few factual errors which should get corrected - and so, some minor edits for future printings have thus been done. It's still essentially the same book.)

CHAPTER 1
MAX TOOTS HIS ROOTS

By the time Max Linder died in 1925, he arguably held a position as the longest-lasting icon of his medium. Having become a household name in France some sixteen years prior as the dashing dandy "Max," he had remained the most enduring persona in films up to his tragic death. Charlie Chaplin and Harold Lloyd had surpassed him in worldwide popularity for sure, but no less did Max still enthrall viewers on occasion, having starred in two films just a year before his passing. Even as his health deteriorated towards the end of his life, causing his public appearances to become decidedly sporadic, his life and whereabouts received an amount of coverage in the press accorded no other movie star whose best work was done before World War I.

Max's claim to have come from a theatrical family has been repeated, and believed, in many retrospectives on the comedian through the years, including one biographical essay by this author in 2012.[2] To trace any such background in his genealogy proves difficult, however, as the claim finds little support in available sources. Only Max appeared to recall that his parents ever seized a stage, and even then rather vaguely.[3]

As the comedian approached middle-age, perhaps he partly invented a family history for himself, believing that reporters and moviegoers expected him to carry such a heritage? If so, this may not have been an unreasonable assumption on his part. After all, the nineteenth and early twentieth centuries had produced an abundance of first-rate comedians, who famously learned prior to entering puberty how to charm an audience, including Chaplin and Keaton, and for that matter, music hall stars such as Dan Leno, going all the way back to the great clown Joseph Grimaldi. While one cannot be absolutely positive that Max's parents were never involved in any kind of theatrical activities, these must have been quite minor at best. More likely, Max had recognized that a great performer was assumed to be the offspring of performers, and saw no harm in embellishing the truth a bit in sessions for fan magazines.

More believable is his assertion that his parents had initially discouraged their son's acting ambitions. As he loosely described his father and mother as "stage folk," he added that they nonetheless "did not want me to act."[4] Indeed, Jean and Suzanne Leuvielle appear to have had other plans for their second son. Married in the late summer of 1880, the Catholic couple had wished for a few inches of vineyard as their wedding gift. Jean, twenty-two, was the son of a clothes trader; while twenty-year old Suzanne, born Baron, was the daughter of Gabriel, a cooper, and Jeanne (b. Carteyron).

France was in a state of political uncertainty at this time. Following the capture of Emperor Napoleon III during the Battle of Sedan in September 1870, and the subsequent French defeat of Germany the following spring, the debate raged as to whether monarchy should be revived in the country, even after the Third French Republic was officially established in 1875. The Paris Bourse Crash of 1882 resulted in a severe Depression which was to last for years to come. The Leuvielles appear to have been blissfully spared from most of this turbulence, however. Having settled down in the small sea village of Cavernes, located in the commune of Saint-Loubès, Gironde in southwestern France, their plantation of grapevines expanded so as to secure a considerable livelihood in the years to come, with the family residing in a stately, two-story brick mansion.

In June 1881, Suzanne gave birth to a son, Maurice Leuvielle. An international rugby champion at eighteen, Maurice would eventually settle on a career related to that of his parents, studying to become a winemaker. Two and a half years later, Maurice was blessed with a little brother, when on December 16, 1883, Gabriel Leuvielle was born. The child would, apparently, go by the name of "Max" from early on.*

Foreshadowing a life that was to be plagued with various physical ailments, Max fell victim to a severe cholera infection while a small child. The fifth known outbreak of the feared pandemic had erupted in India in 1881, spreading to Asia and Africa before reaching France and several other European countries, claiming an estimated total of 250,000 lives in Europe alone within the next fifteen years.[5] Children were especially vulnerable. Young Max fortunately survived, by his own account thanks to a slightly eccentric suggestion from the family physician, who seems to have ordered Jean and Suzanne to let their child rest in the roomy oven of the village baker.[6] The heat from the oven—very carefully regulated by the baker, we must trust—supposedly brought the infection down to a manageable level.

Still more distress struck the family, when their plantation was attacked by grape phylloxera in the spring of 1888. At this point Jean and Suzanne seriously considered immigrating to America to start life anew, going so far as to embark on a trip to New York in search for propitious offers. The children stayed home with grandmother Jeanne. In the end, nothing more became of these plans, Maud Linder reports, as it was discovered that the French vines could be replaced with American plants, which were sturdier and thus resistant to the phylloxera. While in New York, Suzanne had given birth to Gérard Leuvielle. She and Jean happily returned home with a third son in their arms.

Two years later, the three brothers were blessed with a sister, Marcelle, to whom Max was to develop a particular affection.

---

* Max's presumed year of birth has tended to vary in sources. 1882 is mentioned in Walderkranz's book, and Max once claimed his birth to have occurred in 1885 (in a 1923 interview). However, his daughter, Maud, consistently states the year to have been 1883, even showing Max's birth certificate in her documentary *The Man in the Silk Hat* (1983). Also, while Max's initial forename has often been given as Gabriel-Maximillien, his birth certificate only lists him "Gabriel Leuvielle." However, in said documentary Maud maintains that he'd "call himself Max all his life." Since Maud calls her father Max when dealing with his childhood, I will do so, too, for simplicity's sake.

CHAPTER 2
MAX ENGAGED ON STAGE

Given the unlikelihood that Jean and Suzanne had ever been people of the stage to any significant degree, it is hard to say for certain at what point young Max's passion for the footlights first blistered. In contrast to many other entertainers of the same era, he was not born on a stage in any literal or metaphorical sense. Yet, as an adult, he made sure to point out in one brief autobiographical essay dated July 1913 that the inclination had hit him quite early. He recalled that "[f]rom my earliest childhood, my family discovered in me the irresistible vocation of the theater."[7] Maud attests that young Max is reported to have built "a real little scene at the bottom of the [family] garden, invent[ing] texts and play[ing] comedy to his little comrades."[8] On another occasion, he recalled his "dramatic instincts" to have been "awakened by a Punch and Judy show" at the age of four.[9]

Indeed, there is no reason to doubt that Max was drawn toward the extravaganza of drama and comedy while still a young child. The Leuvielles, like any other middleclass family of the period, surely attended performances that came to town from time to time, regardless of the family's own origins. Again, Maud confirms that the commune of Saint-Loubés was not deprived of entertainment: concerts and dance parties were regularly organized.[10] Max also eagerly attended puppet shows, although in that regard he hardly differed from most children of his generation.

Lycée de Talence . . . .

Max's initial interest in theater became all the more pronounced during his first year at the boarding school of Talence. With a population of about 8,000 people at the time of his first year, Talence was among the largest suburbs to the city of Bordeaux. Jean and Suzanne seem to have enrolled their thirteen-year-old son at the school in an attempt to improve his conduct, since Max reportedly had developed a habit of skipping class. The youngster's attention to academic studies remained slight. It proved challenging to raise his interest in school-related chores. He was, on the other hand, popular with girls. More than half a century later, a classmate would recall to his daughter that teenage Max had frequently gotten up at night and swiftly escaped by his window, climbing down to the ground floor, where he had an "appointment with a charming girl . . . who was the daughter of the headmaster."[11]

Most importantly, Max appears to have gotten his first taste of performing at this time, forming theater groups seemingly on his own initiative. Yet, his parents still appeared unconvinced by their son's ambitions. By twenty-first century standards, Jean and Suzanne's restraint toward Max's yearnings may strike some as callous, but their foremost rationale may have been a fear that his lust for the stage would go at the expense of an education, which, after all, was far from commonplace in France at the time. The profession of *acting* also tended to be held in lower regard at the time than today; actress Sarah Bernhardt may have enticed her share of adoring crowds, but more often than not, "players" were rather associated with the sinful detriments of waterholes and other hangouts. Max's stubbornness would prove fruitful in the end, resulting in an extraordinary career, but this was hardly something that his parents could have been expected to foresee with any certainty.

Accounts vary as to what, exactly, Jean and Suzanne expected of their son, beyond earning decent grades at school. He may very well have been envisaged to endorse the same profession as themselves, as has sometimes been implied. For a time the youngster actually considered to become an artist instead, though not for long: "Without telling my parents, I took up painting," Max recalled, "and, with what I thought [to be] my greatest masterpiece, I went to see a well-known painter. 'Yes indeed,' said the [painter], gazing critically at my piece of work, 'it certainly looks promising. But you will never become a second Raphael!'"[12] That, presumably, was that. The vocation of the theater bolstered.

. . . and Conservatoire Muncipal de Bordeaux

Finally, after taking acting lessons in secret through the help of family friend Dr. Ducan, Max decided the time was ripe for him to follow a path of his own in life, and so he entered, at barely eighteen years of age, the Conservatoire Muncipal de Bordeaux, presumably after a meticulous consultation with his parents. They agreed, at last, though quite definitely with reluctance.

Established in the mid-nineteenth century for higher education in music, Bordeaux's respected Conservatory also provided lessons in other arts—drama included. In stark contrast to his years at Talence, Max now turned out to be an attentive student, eager as he was to enhance his abilities as a performer. He developed a particular bond with teacher Adrien Caillard, who, according to Maud, appears to have been the one to give Max "secret lessons" prior to his admission at the Conservatory. Relationships to other teachers were more tense, though, as Max wished for more opportunities to perform while they thought he lacked experience.

Thankfully, second term's end turned out a success. On July 7, 1903, Max seized First Prize in Drama during the Conservatory's annual school competition, held at Bordeaux's Grand Theater, and he garnered Second Prize in Comedy.[13] While it has been reported that this contest marked his graduation from the school, Maud maintains that it only concluded his first year, and that he was in fact dismissed from the school by second year's start due to more quarrels with his teachers.[14]

Max Lacerda enters

At any rate, the first few months after Max's departure resulted in some promising offers. Most notably, he was to spend the remainder of the year appearing in at least three classic plays at Théâtre des Arts Bordeaux, including Molière's *Les Précieuses ridicules* and *Les Fourberies de Scapin*, as well as Rossini's *Barber of Seville*. The pay was supposed to have been "extremely poor," however, the hard work considered.[15] Also, his parents were still lukewarm in their enthusiasm. Even this late, they appear to have needed persuasion once more to let their son go on with his dreams. Once again, they did relent, but with their usual unease; Max's father so much so that, apparently, he demanded of his son not to be billed under the family name. Prior to entering Théâtre des Arts Bordeaux, the aspiring actor settled on a pseudonym he deemed appropriate: that of Max *Lacerda*.

By spring 1904, Max had moved to Paris, procuring a contract at Théâtre de l'Ambigu-Comique, possibly through the help of his earlier teacher, Caillard. First founded in 1769, de l'Ambigu-Comique may not have been the most prominent of Parisian stages, but it still carried a sort of legendary status, having endured several renovations, as well as a huge fire in its history. (The theater was to survive for decades after Max's days there, finally closing down in 1966.)

By now a professional actor with credentials to show, Max soon discovered the *footlights* to be a ruthless business. Around the same time as his engagement at de l'Ambigu-Comique came about, he presented himself for Paris' Conservatory of Music and Declamation—whose studies also included drama—but without success. He was to try again twice in subsequent years, with no more luck.

"That's my name!"

Nonetheless, Max staggered on. In October, 1904, another performer's sudden absence led him to be handed the role of a captain in the play, *Le tour du monde d'un enfant de Paris*. Penned by Ernest Morel, the staging was received approvingly. Max's next part, presumably his first "official" work at Théâtre de l'Ambigu-Comique would prove an historical event in hindsight. Debuting on December 3, 1904, *Le crime d'Aix* marked the first time the name of "Max Linder" was used in the credits, according both to Maud and Georg Renken.[16] "Lacerda" was hence put to rest.

There is some debate as to how Max landed on the name of Linder. The most oft-told version, repeated by Maud, recounts how Max, while on a stroll with his sister, passed a shoe-store in Bordeaux boasting LINDER in large letters. "That's my name!" he is supposed to have exclaimed.[17] However, film historian Jack Spears believed the name "Max Linder" to have likely been a nod to the actors Max Dearly and Marcelle Lender,[18] whom Max knew well at the time. However, as Max seems to have taken on his forename while still a youngster, we can probably omit Dearly from this equation, while Marcelle Lender seems a more plausible guess as far as "Linder" is concerned.

(Incidentally, Dearly was to eventually embark on a rather notable film career of his own after sound came in, appearing in Raymond Bernard's five-hour adaptation of Les misérables (1934). Lender was likely best-known for an 1896 staging of Hervé's operetta Chilpéric.)

While he never had his surname legally changed from Leuvielle, Max was to employ the alias of Linder throughout his professional life. Although obviously unintentional on his part, the new pseudonym may arguably have played a factor in his eventual rise to worldwide fame, Linder being a reasonably universal name and less unmistakably French than Lacerda or Leuvielle.

A household name Max Linder was not as of yet, however. The New Year took off with a misfire at Théâtre de l'Ambigu: Camille Audigier and Paul Géry's play, La conquête de l'air, closed after four fleeting performances, Max having played the minor role of Santa-Fé. More successful was the staging of Adolphe d'Ennery's drama, Les deux orphelines, which premiered on January 20, 1905 and apparently ran for 53 performances. According to Renken, Max initially played a character named "de Mailly" in the play, but was given the role of "Marquis de Presles" when the staging was temporarily resurrected later in the year.[19]

Mysterious medium

Linder's commitment to Théâtre de l'Ambigu had indeed resulted in a busy schedule for the actor. Although he no doubt would have preferred larger roles than the theater could grant him, the experience was surely valuable. In February, he played "Beaumensil" in another drama penned by Adolphe d'Ennery, Paillasse. Three weeks later, the theater had another hit with Pierre Berton's play, La belle marseillaise, with Max as "Caulaincourt." Spring came with a staging of Gaston Marot's Les Aventures de Thomas Plumepatte, in which Max went by the fitting name of "Maxwel." The summer provided a success with Gardel-Hervé and Maurice Varret's drama, La bande à Fifi, with Max playing "Ildefonse."

More stage plays were still to come within the remainder of 1905, but by then, Max had also made his first fumbling steps toward plays of another, more mysterious kind.

To make ends meet, he appears to have posed for postcards while engaged at Théâtre de l'Ambigu. However, an additional job proposal was soon to come his way. Exactly how it happened is unclear; but one way or the other, in the summer of 1905, Max was admitted to the flourishing *studio de cinema*, Pathé Frères. Maud allows for passing mention of Max Dearly's claim that Pathé Frères had originally sought out *him*, whereby Dearly had declined and suggested his friend Max Linder instead.[20] This proves hard to corroborate. In any event, it is unlikely that anyone at Pathé Frères had taken an interest in Max by seeing him onstage—as was to be the case with Charlie Chaplin years later in America—considering how relatively minor Max's roles were at that point. To assume that he was somehow recommended to the film studio, be it by Dearly or someone else, may not seem unreasonable after all, especially since he was to play leading roles at Pathé Frères more or less from day one.

CHAPTER 3
MAX THE CAREER PIONEER

Film was, of course, not yet widely acknowledged as an art form in 1905, or hardly even a potential one, but budding creativity blossomed no less among its pioneers. Certainly the public's huge interest in the new medium had become more or less unquestionable by this point, a decade having passed since the Lumiére brothers famously held what is generally considered the first "official" screening of motion pictures at Boulevard des Capucines in Paris, December 1895. (The oft-repeated legend that audiences for a time tired of the flickers due to a lack of new innovations seems doubtful at closer distance, according to Rune Walderkranz.)

Even so, what eventually came to be regarded as *the* medium of the twentieth century largely remained a guilty pleasure to middleclass audiences, and an internal crisis had begun to develop within the industry over the lack of an effective distribution system. The unorganized manner in which most early films were produced also led to programs being often rather monotonous, as filmmakers tended to unabashedly borrow concepts and ideas from one another (one famous example being the many plagiarized versions of Cecil Hepworth's *Rescued by Rover* (1905), which was originally produced in Britain and notable for its use of fluid, expressive camera shots).

This is not to say that there was an absence of ingenuity to be found, for quite the contrary is true. Georges Méliès (1861-1938) in France, and Edwin S. Porter (1870-1941) in the United States, may be the most well-known of these earliest pioneers today, but a wealth of other directors also helped, in sum, to establish film as a self-contained means of expression in these formative years, contending its initial reputation as a subpar (and "fun-looking") alternative to the stage. Subtle, new directorial techniques arrived with increasing frequency. Prior to the invention of modernized projectors that gave a less flickering, more viewer-friendly projection around 1911, most films were "one-reelers," which means that the entire film fit on a single 1,000-ft reel of 35 mm film, and, when shown at the correct speed, ran for approximately 12 minutes. Attempts at feature-length films that used multiple 1,000-ft reels to tell a longer story, were few and far between initially. For a single admission ticket, audiences were usually treated to a program of several silent one- or two-reel films, typically a short drama, a comedy, and, a bit later on, sometimes a newsreel. In the absence of "sound," pictures were duly accompanied by live music on a single piano or organ, a small ensemble, and eventually, a large orchestra at the more prominent theaters.

Still, the need for more professionalism had become sorely felt by the early 1900s, and it was especially in this regard that the Pathé brothers, Jacques, Émile, Théophile, and Charles Pathé at the forefront, proved to be truly invaluable as pioneers.

Butcher son

Not unlike the case of Max Linder, there had been little to no indication initially that Charles Pathé or any of his brothers would make a name for themselves as leading figures of an ascending mass medium. Born into a family of butchers in 1863, based in the commune of Chevry-Cossigny in north-central France, it had been taken for granted that Charles would pursue their parents' trade of work. He turned out to be a restless young man, however, perhaps eager to earn acclaim unlikely to be accorded him in the butcher business, and clearly captivated by the boundless level of technical advancements that surged European societies in the late nineteenth century. After a series of failed business stints overseas along with his siblings, Charles reportedly had to settle for the job of a solicitor's clerk for a time. Nonetheless, the ambition to stand out in a field remained alive even as he approached middle-age.

By most accounts, it was in the summer of 1894 that thirty-one-year old Charles finally happened upon the apparatus that would prove to be the door opener he had likely searched for. While at home in the Paris suburb of Vincennes, where his family by now had moved, he witnessed a demonstration of Thomas Edison's phonograph. Though it may seem unlikely that the phonograph was a completely alien device to Charles, given his interest in technology, along with the fact that Edison's first version of the machine had been launched all the way back in 1877, the invention still drew the attention of a novelty in most crowds. Intrigued, Charles is said to have secured for himself an assortment of phonographs. Barely a year later, film historian Richard Abel notes, his newfound enthusiasm (and arguably shrewdness) led him to issue bogus versions of an invention for which Edison was also the recognized creator—not the phonograph, but the kinetoscope.[21] Predating "regular" movie projectors by some crucial years, the kinetoscope enabled peephole showings of brief motion picture snippets to individual viewers. (In fairness, as is often noted, one may understand that the Pathé brothers could not resist to utilize the fact that Edison's American patent on the kinetoscope did not apply in Europe.)

Les Frères

After yet another year, in 1896, the brothers felt sufficiently confident so that Société Pathé Frères was launched. Abel reports that the brothers hired one Henri Joseph Joly to develop a device that borrowed heavily from the Lumières' recently unveiled cinématographe, but the collaboration proved unfruitful and was short-lived.[22] Far more promising did their partnership with factory proprietor Claude Grivolas turn out; by late 1897, Pathé's endeavor had, with the cooperation of Grivolas, been transformed into a valuable business corporation. During these first few years, the phonograph remained the company's primary asset and source of income, but this was to change in due time.

The major turn for Pathé occurred, historians agree, shortly after the Paris World Exhibition of 1900, as Charles witnessed firsthand the popularity of his company's hand-colored motion pictures among onlookers.[23] Certainly Pathé Frères' interest in the new medium had manifested itself well before the Exhibition, Charles having produced dozens of brief film snippets all the way back to 1896, but it seems to be correct that the company decided to make le cinéma their first priority around this time. Their hitherto unassuming facility was expanded into a professional studio within the next few years. Based in Vincennes, the new factory allowed for production of films on an industrial scale.

Fierce empire

Prior stage manager Ferdinand Zecca (1864-1947) proved most useful to Pathé Frères during these early years, perhaps more for his quantity than anything else. Having been responsible for the successful marquee of Pathé's films at the Paris Exhibition, Zecca soon became one of the most prolific directors at the company. Though renowned for an ample productivity more than outstanding imagination in retrospect, Zecca's films did evince a sharpness as far as audience perception was concerned. If his work lacked a strong overall identity of the kind that made wizards such as Méliès and Porter stand out, his basic cinematic understanding as a director is still noteworthy considering how pubescent the medium of film still was at this point.

Another distinguished director early on at Pathé, whose talents would eventually contribute to the worldwide breakthrough of Max Linder himself, was a certain Lucien Nonguet (1868-1920). Under Zecca's supervision, Nonguet helped direct one of Pathé's most notorious successes of the early 1900s, *La vie et la passion de Jésus Christ* (*The Story of Christ*). This did not in any way mark the first time the life and fate of Jesus was adapted to film, for sure; the Lumière-brothers had, among others, dramatized the event as far back as 1897, creating quite a ballyhoo in the process. However, Pathé's take on the subject did stand out in its day. Though their film was made available in several lengths and formats, the most well-known version was released in 1903 at approximately 40 minutes, a near-epic running-time for a photoplay of that time. In its entirety, the film may be said to have cemented Pathé's impressive path of progress at the turn of the century. The company's output enjoyed a massive spread, soon reaching across the Atlantic, as well.

Despite some shots at extended productions, however, the vast majority of Pathé's films were brief, usually running at less than one reel. Always on the lookout for new plots and twists, directors freely used and built upon the tried-and-true formulas of varieté and melodrama. While far from an island to themselves within the industry—around the same time, Porter was famously laying the ground for the upcoming Western genre in the United States, for one thing—Pathé's clever, systematized distribution and marketing of films made the company hard to beat for overall impact. Throughout the first decade of the 1900s, Charles Pathé easily ruled the fiercest empire in the business.

An unbilled unknown—Max Linder enters

The wide variety of players that inhabited Pathé's earliest films were unbilled, effectively unrecognizable from one release to another, as was the custom in all film production at the time, in Europe and the United States alike. Film actors were still not perceived as "real" actors per se, comedians being no exception. Thus, when "Max Linder" Leuvielle made his screen debut in the brief comic film, *La première sortie d'un collégien (His First Night Out)*, directed by Louis Gasnier and released on August 5, 1905, audiences had no way of discerning the newcomer's identity, nor would they have cared to know it at that point. Max likely shared the public's indifference at first. Though the new assignment did provide a welcome additional paycheck—he later recalled to have been paid 40F a week during his first stint at Pathé,[24] though other sources claim 20F[25]—*le théâtre* prevailed as his primary focus for at least another year. Whether or not he viewed the opportunity to work in an infant medium as slightly more ceremonious than posing for postcards, his cinematic output would remain quite sporadic for still a while to come. Max's later recollection that he had appeared in a new film "every day" during his first years at Pathé was clearly exaggeration[26] (though it is possible that the comedian, with this claim, meant to bring attention to the fact that nearly all films in the early 1900s were shot within a few days, which was certainly true).

Sporadic or not, Pathé must have sensed Max's potential from the start, or they would not have let their novice receive a leading role thus early. The scenario of *La première* features Max as a youngster, dressed in a schoolboy's uniform, who has tricked his father and mother into—separately—lending him money. Later on, a happy gathering with some fellow students is spoiled due to a disagreement over a bill, resulting in a brawl. Back home at night, the young man receives a deserved scolding from his parents. Finis.

Max's role as that of an inexperienced teenager was to be repeated in subsequent films. Indeed, initial attempts to establish a comic identity for the comedian seem to have largely taken advantage of his youthful appearance. Logical though this decision may have struck his first handful of directors—he was only approaching twenty-two, after all—it only worked up to a point. Nothing really sets the young man apart from Pathé's wardrobe of other unnamed funnymen in these first few screen sketches, though an elementary talent is apparent, for sure.

Less than a week after the virgin showing of *La Première*, another brief film with Max in the lead may have been released, this time directed by Zecca and Nonguet, entitled *Dix femmes pour un mari* (*Ten Wives for One Husband*). As no copy of this sketch is known to exist and few reviews have surfaced, his rumored appearance in it has been hard to verify. A synopsis reveals the film to be about a bachelor of thirty-two, who has decided to place an ad for a wife to himself in the local paper, only to be overwhelmed by a massive response from a horde of females, and so he ultimately finds it best to escape them all.[27] A well-known intrigue that was to frequent film comedy for years to come, this story was, of course, brought to another level entirely in Buster Keaton's classic feature *Seven Chances* (1925). [2020s update: The film is in fact still extant and does not seem to feature Max, certainly not in the leading role.]

More certain is Max's assumed appearance in *La Rencontre imprévue* (*Unforeseen Meeting*), another brief film probably released in August; although lost today, at least one still picture seems to have survived. Its title likely borrowed from Christoph W. Gluck's comic opera of 1763, Max here appears to have played a youngster courting the same mistress as his unsuspecting father.

Still stage-struck

Any impression that Max at first viewed his cinematic career as nothing grander than an extra buck, is strengthened by the fact that his first span at Pathé apparently came to a pause after these first two or three films, while his stage career sustained. Returning to Théâtre de l'Ambigu in September, he was given the role of "Tom Bluff" in Maurice Lefèvre's play, *Le crime d'un fils*. This play, incidentally, seems to have been adapted to film at least twice during the silent era; but not, alas, with Max Linder. It closed down after a few weeks. In October, he appeared as "Poplard" in Jules Mary and George Grisier's drama, *Le Régiment*—again, not a popular hit. Six weeks on, Théâtre de l'Ambigu was no doubt relieved to have a success with Alexandre Arquillière's play, *La grande famille*, with Max personifying "Officer Rondet." This play ran well into the New Year, gaining favorable reviews, but though Max's roles were sufficiently big for his efforts to be noticed, his years at Théâtre de l'Ambigu had not made him a headliner.

CHAPTER 4
MAX'S SUREFIRE ATTIRE

There is little reason to believe that Max bragged about his recent screen spell to his stage companions. More likely, he knew well to shut up about it. The early months of 1906 seem to have brought no new screen credits, while he continued to occupy the stage of Théâtre de l'Ambigu in smaller parts. Following the closure of *La grande famille*'s successful run, a five-act dramatization on Napoleon Bonaparte premiered in March. Bearing the patriotic title of *Pour sa patrie* (*For His Homeland*), the play covered the historical period leading up to the Napoleonic Wars and onward, featuring such important figures as General Józef Poniatowski and, as portrayed by Max, Ambassador Dominique-Georges-Frédéric Dufour de Pradt. Again, not an insignificant role, for sure, but Napoleon it was not. The play on Bonaparte was tepidly received, however, and reached its end after just a few performances.

Another stint

Less than a month later, Linder appeared as "Lemiret" in Maurice Landay's drama, *La tourmente*, a staging that received a glowing review in *Le Journal du Dimanche*, though with barely a mention of Max Linder.[28] It may have been just as well, though. Following eight performances of *La tourmente*, the actor's time at Théâtre de l'Ambigu was effectively over. Instead, he was to spend the next few months primarily reviving his screen career, once again on Pathé's lot. With more than half a year having passed, presumably, since his first fling with motion pictures ended, had Max perhaps regained an interest in the peculiar medium, however elusive that interest had seemed in the first place? It may in fact have been an act out of necessity more than anything else, but Pathé appears to have welcomed him back without qualms.

In truth, it is possible that Max had maintained some contact with the studio amidst his theatrical obligations; the repeated claim that he often appeared as an extra in films early on could imply as much. In any case, the short film, *Les étudiants de Paris (The Paris Students)* marked his return in a starring role onscreen, first brought to the public on May 27, 1906. Directed by Harry Ray, Max here once again plays an unruly youngster, who this time is sent by his father to Paris to study art, only to discover that he much prefers partying to painting. It is a plausible guess that Max drew some inspiration for this sketch from his own upbringing, though it bears mentioning that Pathé's comedies nearly swarmed with similar scenarios in this period. On the very same day, another film also starring Max was released, entitled *Julot va dans le monde (Bill Goes to a Party)*, with the comedian playing a man-about-town named Julot.

Persistent perseverance

Clues to Max's personal life during this phase are slight. After his schooling at Bordeaux's Conservatory, his parents had likely come sufficiently to terms with their son's ambitions to not stand in his way, but as he alternated between billed minor roles onstage and unbilled leading roles onscreen, his story was not yet that of a boy-made-good. Starring in one more short film during the early summer, released as *La puce gênante (The Troublesome Flea)* on July 2, his name was still unknown to movie audiences, while the stage remained his true vocation.

His persistence was about to pay off. Finally declining an offer (for which he seems to have said yes initially) at Théâtre Réjane, Max instead joined Théâtre des Variétés by late autumn. Well onboard, the new recruit was handed the role of "Beurier" in Robert de Flers' comic play, *Miquette et sa mere*, resulting in a considerable success. Eventually adapted to film by legendary director H.G. Clouzot in 1950, the play tells the story of a stage-struck young girl, who endures much adversity for her dreams. Max could no doubt have identified with this plot to a degree, but his role in the play was relatively minor also this time around. However, concurrently with his part in *Miquette*, the actor was also chosen for the role of "Chambly" in the one-act play, *La main droite*, debuting on November 4, 1906. With this, Max finally made it as leading man onstage. The play was deemed a "well-formed genre comedy" in the press, and Max received some passing praise along with the other performers.[29]

Surprisingly, Pathé offered at least one more film with Max in the lead before year's end, despite his being preoccupied with two stage hits at this time: released in mid-December and directed by Gasnier, *Le pendu* (*Attempted Suicide*) has Max attempting to commit suicide by hanging. Some viewers may understandably find this premise much too macabre to enjoy, as Max actually succeeds in the somber act, or at least very nearly so. For minutes hanging lifelessly beneath a branch with a shattered look on his face, he is finally rescued by police in the upmost nick of time. Unlike the later comic suicide attempts by Harold Lloyd in *Haunted Spooks* (1920) and Buster Keaton in *Hard Luck* (1921), the act is here performed nearly dead-serious, with zero gags to make up for it, and thus our distance to the execution remains arguably too slight for us to laugh at it. However, upon the film's release in the United States, one reviewer in *Variety* praised the brief scene, suggesting it to be most of all a "travesty" on French police.[30] Sure enough, the cops prove quite incompetent, as they set off to save Max, obviously more concerned with formalities than the young man's life.

Travesty or not, *Le pendu* is perhaps most notable today for displaying Max in a role akin to the one he was to make his trademark, sporting dark bowler and light suit. He is plainly approaching the *gentleman boulevardier* of his later films. (Incidentally, the comedian appears to have done a remake of this film years later in 1914 by the same title. Unfortunately, a comparison is not feasible, as the latter version is thought to be lost.)

Max's screen appearances were still rather irregular, however, and not yet confined to starring roles. Also, in late 1906, the very brief film, *Lèvres collées* (*Joined Lips*), had him do a cameo appearance as a customer at a post office. At any rate, the comedian seems to have taken his work at Pathé more seriously from this time on, and so, probably, did the studio. As a matter of fact, a few of the "nameless mugs" of Pathé's farces were now soon to be identified by nicknames, although the progress would be slow indeed.

CHAPTER 5
MAX EXCEEDS DEED

Nearly as important as Pathé's early attention to distribution, one may argue in hindsight, was their realization that it paid off to showcase recurring *personalities* in films. "Personalities" may be too flattering a noun, though. Starting around 1907, some very few diffuse comic performers began to gain recognition among audiences with film after film. Quite likely, Pathé Frères came to this discovery by simply turning their heads to other media for a moment. While the movies still only featured anonymous, unbilled performers in the first few years of the 1900s, Vaudeville was rich with acclaimed star comedians: Dan Leno, Marie Lloyd, Harry "Little Tich" Relph, the French clown Marceline, and so on. So was, for that matter, the modern comic strip, which was slowly finding its way to Europe from the "yellow press" of the United States.

With more than a century having passed since Pathé's first few nicknamed comedians emerged, it would perhaps seem wise not to attribute the seed of this development to one performer in particular. As stated above, the upgrowth of "film personalities" was quite gradual—and likely haphazard, to a degree—during these initial years. Even so, one mirth maker has, in fact, been widely acknowledged as the very first such film personality.

Deed's Boireau

Presumably born in 1879,[*] André Chapuis had behind him a career as a performer in circus and varieté when he was first hired by Pathé's studio in 1906, by which time he had already adopted the pseudonym of "André Deed." Unlike Max, Deed was not thoroughly unfamiliar with the medium upon his arrival, having previously appeared in some of Méliès' films. Once admitted, he soon came to star in a series of film sketches as the clownish character, Boireau, one of his first titles being *Boireau déménage* (*Boireau On The Move*), released May 1906. No doubt thanks to

---

[*] Some sources say 1884. These clowns sure weren't shy about discarding a few years if they could, but February 22, 1879 is most often listed.

Pathé's worldwide distribution, along with the deft decision to often work Boireau's name into a film's title, Deed quickly found himself a popular comedian to an audience far outreaching his circus days. With "Boireau" being so very French-sounding, however, Deed's character typically went by various epithets across the borders—"Jim" in the United States—although in some countries, including Norway, he seems to have actually maintained his original nickname.[31]

Though it is questionable if André Deed in 1906-1907 should be regarded a true *movie star* (more on this below), his Boireau may be rightly labeled as the first screen character to have generated a "following." With his brief farces, such as *Les apprentissages du Boireau*, *Boireau roi des voleurs*, and *Boireau lutteur* (all 1907), he very arguably marked the first instance of a film performer rivaling the importance of his studio. After all, thus far it had been the name of *Pathé* (if anything) that mattered to audiences and exhibitors. His popularity eventually led to offers elsewhere. In 1909, he abandoned Pathé (and Boireau) for a series of films produced in Italy, renaming his character to "Cretinetti" in the process. "Cretinetti" became known as "Gribouille" in France; "Foolshead" in the United States; "Leman" in Norway and Sweden. Deed remained in Italy for two years before returning to France, reviving Boireau. Perhaps surprisingly, his international fame did persist well into the 1910s; screenings of his films were announced with relative frequency in the American press as late as 1915.[32] Even so, one article in a Norwegian paper of the year before (incidentally devoted to the whereabouts of Max Linder) declares his popularity to have "faded."[33] Later in the decade, Deed's filmography becomes quite spotty, although he kept on doing occasional screen appearances nearly up to his death in 1940.

Enticing name

Deed's popularity was a fact well before Max Linder's breakthrough, for sure, despite his having arrived at Pathé a year later. It may be safely assumed, then, that the success of the Boireau series (directly or indirectly) enhanced Pathé's interest in Max as a leading comedian. In the end, however, to declare Deed a "movie star" prior to Max's rise still sounds dubious to this author.

Enticing though Boireau's name was to early moviegoers—no small feat in and of itself—press coverage that I have been able to find does not attest to anything resembling a *mass hysteria* level of idolization. Earth-shattering stardom among entertainers was still confined to the luminaries of the stage. Of course, it should be stressed that the very idea of showcasing a recurrent character in a film series was completely untrodden territory at the time of Deed/Boireau's debut. So, if he was not a true movie star by later standards, he does at least qualify as its primal precursor.

As a performer, Deed arguably comes off as somewhat indistinguishable today. While no doubt a capable mime, his gestures tend to be quite broad; his training from circus and varieté is evident in this regard. He is less of a "character" than he is a vessel for the hapless scenarios in which he finds himself from week to week—a "fool's head," in other words. Based on what the author has been able to view, his films uphold a solid average standard; they're generally pleasant, but often rather mechanical, with not all that much individuality to make them stand out. Audiences were understandably amused by Deed's antics, but I find it hard to believe that he ever *bonded* with his public. He was basically a funny man, a cartoon character. Nothing wrong with that. Regardless, the early success of Deed, along with some very few other film jesters such as the Italian clown Roméo Bosetti, did foreshadow Max's own popular leap, which was by now lurking.

Angered Karno

With the success of the play, *La main droite* still fresh on Max's mind, more film credits piled up in winter 1907. One of his first efforts of the year brought Pathé in trouble, however. Max may or may not have been responsible for this—the film's director is unknown—but the short film, *Au music hall* (At the Music Hall), greatly angered British stage manager Fred Karno. Best-known today as Chaplin's early mentor, the legendary Karno claimed that the film was a cribbing of his music hall sketch, Mumming Birds, and so he pressed charges. Whether or not Karno's complaint had a point, however, this was an age when a portly percentage of all film production consisted of unmasked plagiarism. As the medium was still not taken all that seriously by most, copy-

right violation in films likely bothered few—the courts included.*
Richard Brown notes, in his book *In the Kingdom of the Shadows*, that the adaptation was concluded to "not constitute an infringement" according to the 1833 Dramatic Copyright Act.[34] A letdown to Karno, no doubt, the manager nonetheless found himself in plenty of similar disputes through the years.[35]

Whether or not *Au music hall* qualified as theft—it may have been intended as a travesty—the film does seem to echo Karno's sketch quite a bit. Running at five minutes or so, it presents an intoxicated Max constantly interrupting the performers of an act he has attended. Thought to have been lost for over a century, a copy of the film was unexpectedly found in Mexico in 2014. Other film comedians were to bring this premise to new heights later on (Chaplin, famously, in his *A Night in the Show* (1915), but Max gives an amusing performance, and once again seems to be drawing toward his "classic" persona all the more.

Not quite there

"Gentleman Max" was not yet fully born, however. February saw release of the brief dramatic film, *L'empoisonneuse* (*The Phial of Poison*). Unlike the earlier *Le pendu*, this sketch seems to have been intended as straightforward drama rather than satire. The author has been unable to view the film, but it is said to have involved the poisoning of a lover and a woman getting shot in the head, among other things.[36] Not exactly a gag feast, *Le Pendu* at least ended well. The decision to have Max star in this gloomy scenario (presumably as one of two lovers) may imply that Pathé had not yet figured out how to best make use of his services. His role choices still appear somewhat random, though there is no doubt that he was an adept dramatic actor (as he was to demonstrate again on a few later occasions).

---

* This situation would soon change after the December 7, 1907 release of *Ben Hur* (sic), a one-reel film based on Lew Wallace's best-selling novel, *Ben-Hur: A Tale of the Christ*. The book's publisher, Harper & Brothers, sued Kalem Studios, the Motion Picture Patents Company, and screen adaptation author Gene Gauntier for copyright infringement. The United States Supreme Court ruled against Kalem in 1911. This ruling established a new precedent that all motion picture production companies must first secure the film rights of any previously published work still under copyright before commissioning a screenplay based on that work.

Increasing film credits notwithstanding, Max found time to do at least one more stage production within the year, albeit in a different kind of play. With a first performance held March 3 at Thèâtre des Variétés, *La revue de centenaire* obviously celebrated the theater's centenary.[37] Achieving a total of 114 performances, Max played the double role of a secretary and Napoleonic War General Eugène de Beauharnais.

Following the revue's finish, however, he spent the remainder of 1907 at Pathé's *usine de films*.

CHAPTER 6
MAX STACKS UP

Spring of 1907 brought about the first regular batch of Max Linder films. Though not yet known by name, the rather diminutive "Pathé player" with the well-trimmed moustache was no doubt getting noticed by the public. In particular, one film from this year is repeatedly listed as an early signature work. Within five minutes and ten seconds, *Les débuts d'un patineur* (*Max Learns To Skate*) laid the basis for his soon-to-be iconic character. The sketch is undeniably simple even by the standards of the day, staged in a single setting over nine shots: we see Max arrive at an ice rink, brimming with diligence over a new pair of skates. Dressed in evening clothes (top hat and all), he sets out on the rink only to be overwhelmed by his own inexperience. As he bumbles and stumbles, a few well-meaning passersby try to come to the rescue, but it proves hopeless, all the more so when Max is bombarded with snowballs by a group of rascals. The police having finally intervened, our hero is seen drenched with snow and exhaustion in the last shot, sobbing uncontrollably to the camera as his all-wrecked hat falls to the ground. *Finis.*

Simple, yes—any of Pathé's comedians could have embarked on a miserable skating experience, for sure—but a particular style was on the rise. Max arguably differs from Pathé's other "clowns" of 1907 in that he *isn't* a clown; it is not the sight of his well-dressed dandy that is funny so much as the sight of his well-dressed dandy getting into ill-fated comic settings. This facet of Max's comedy was to become all the more pronounced in succeeding years: that of the basically well-mannered charmer being unluckily exposed to tricky predicaments, a comedy of contrasts, one might say. The character that Max was now well on his way to develop may to this day strike us as surprisingly identifiable, or even "real." This is not to say that he is particularly *complex*—these are five- to ten-minute comedy shorts, after all—but from about 1907 on, he is certainly less of a "burlesque" than his contemporaries at Pathé.

On *Les débuts d'un patineur* (*Max Learns To Skate*), Rune Walderkranz notes: "... an inexperienced roller-skater may do a laughable figure but is made comic through the contrast which his fashionable elegance creates in a thoroughly athletic setting."[38] This particular aspect is prone to be lost on many modern viewers, though. Audiences of 1907 would have immediately recognized the absurdity of a man dressed in top hat entering the ice rink with skates beneath him, but one suspects that a modern public may take for granted that "that's just how people dressed back then."

In 1950, forty-three years after the release of *Les débuts d'un patineur* on March 23, 1907, Pathé director Louis Gasnier recalled to have directed this brief film, in a letter quoted by Maud. What's more, he also claimed this to have been "Max Linder's first film."[39] Maud speculates if Gasnier may have had his memory clouded by the word "débuts" in the film's title. This does perhaps seem most plausible—Gasnier was in his seventies by then—but it may also be possible that he had meant to emphasize that this film was the first to display Max's character *as he came to be known*. To clarify: it had likely *not* been a case of Max having "found" a character on the spot, in the way that one might argue that Chaplin "found" the Tramp quite instantly at Keystone, but based on the films that the author has been able to view, this sketch does indeed seem to have signaled a transition.

Killed for jewelry

Stylistic deviations were still rather frequent, however. On April 26, 1907, Pathé released another short drama with Linder in a role; *Pour un collier* (*All For A Necklace*) seems to follow a quite generic, if gruesome, scenario involving—you guessed it—a costly necklace (and a murder). The author has not been able to track down the film, but a synopsis reads as follows: *"A husband desires to buy a necklace for his wife, but the price is too stiff, [so] the jewels are sent back, leaving the [wife] in a rather bad temper as a consequence. At a friend's house, the [couple] notice the necklace on the throat of their hostess. The [hostess] ... sends her maid to put [the necklace] in her room ... [T]he man follows, and is [admiring] the necklace when the [hostess] enters. He murders her and* goes off with the jewels, and when his wife enters, presents them to her...."⁴⁰ Quite clearly not meant as good-natured fun. If it's any consolation, Max appears not to have played the evildoer here, but the jeweler.

It must have been evident to Pathé that comedy was Max's forte, though. Also in April, *Ah! Quel malheur d'avoir un gendre* (*Mother-in-Law's Visit*) hit the screens, presenting Max, of course, as the son-in-law. This was not to be the last time the comedian, who in real life would remain a bachelor for many more years to come, poked fun at the phenomenon of domestic life, in-laws included. A comic sketch involving him and a pair of new, all too tight shoes was also released the same month as *Chaussure trop étroite* (*The Joys of Tight Boots*).

Long hours

How Max spent his free time between all professional obligations during this period is anybody's guess. Whereas he was to give some hints as to his private life in later interviews, as far as I can see he was still not sought out for press portraits in 1907. His face may have become well-known by then, but he was still "one of the nameless ones." Most likely, he found himself immersed in his work at most hours. Days at Pathé's factory could be long indeed, but this was—by all accounts—his dream job, after all.

The most notable of all the unexpected roles that Max undertook within 1907, was probably that of a *commedia dell'arte* character in Albert Capellani's fantasy-film *La légende de Polichinelle*. To say that the role was unexpected is a bit misleading, though. It may strike us modern-day viewers as such, but it can be assumed that Max was well-versed in the tradition of commedia dell'arte from his years onstage. Released June 14, the film casts him (disguised beyond recognition) in the role of Pulcinella. The copy currently available runs at about eight minutes; however, in an American ad for the film, it is advertised as having the "unusual length" of "over 1,340 feet" (ca. 408 meter),⁴¹ suggesting it to have been several minutes longer upon release. In any event, within the surviving copy, Pulcinella saves his sweetheart, who's been bewitched into a doll, from a group of bluebloods at a gloomy castle. He sees her (literally) break to pieces after a blaze, but in the end manages to have her "repaired" into a breathing entity again (phew!).

This nicely-tinted film was a definite departure from the comedy (and drama) in which Linder had wholly operated thus far at Pathé, but it was not an abnormal creation for the studio *en masse*. Often noted for its similarities to the films of Méliès, *La légende de Polichinelle* does indeed include some fine "special effects" and a fanciful (if occasionally macabre) story, though tenfold similar films had been made at Pathé and elsewhere by this point. Despite being the lead, Max is quite anonymous amidst the fantasy. The film was obviously not meant to show off any of its actors, but rather have the story and special effects carry it through (another parallel to Méliès).

(Incidentally, *La légende de Polichinelle* was released as *Harlequin's Story* in the United States, likely due to Harlequin's wider fame.)

Skirts & balloons

Mid-summer came and proved equally productive. In *Les péripéties d'un amant* (*Lover's Ill Luck*), Max plunged into a role that any self-respecting silent comedian was to do at one point or another—that of a man in drag. Max is having a good time with his secret mistress, when the woman's husband suddenly arrives home. Escaping the wrath of the jealous spouse, our hero fetches a few of his girlfriend's duds and flees the scene. Once outside, however, he quickly attracts a mob of eager males, resulting in a hefty race.

A day later, on July 6, 1907, no less than *two* new Max Linder films saw release, both directed by Nonguet. One of them, *Les débuts d'un aéronaute* (*The Aeronaut's First Appearance*), was hailed in British press as "one of the best subjects [Pathé] ha[s] yet produced."[42] As its title suggests, this sketch takes place mostly above ground, having Max enter an arising air balloon. The expedition proves disastrous, however, as the aircraft winds up crushing a rooftop and drags along with it a newsstand and a doghouse, among other things. The film's special effects are slickly done, and the sketch remains amusing to this day, although Max's acting tends to be best realized in more lightly physical scenarios, in my opinion (whereas Nonguet's comedies often follow a rather mechanical framework).

The other film released that day bears an equally revealing title: *Le domestique hypnotiseur* (*The Servant Hypnotist*) has Max's servant trying to break off his master's engagement through hypnosis. British critics had high praise to offer also this time around; "[t]he acting throughout the scenes is of the cleverest [kind] and the ludicrous incidents are very numerous."[43] Although still unnamed on-screen, Max's confidence must've escalated during this phase.

Pathé released at least two more films with Max Linder before summer's end. In *Pitou, bonne d'enfants* (*Private Atkins Minds a Baby*), his character bears the name of Pitou (or "Atkins" in English), a soldier who's been "left in charge of a baby on a seat in the park by his sweetheart ... and walks up and down trying to keep [the child] in a good temper."[44] Mishaps then occur, as Pitou places the baby on a wheelbarrow while saluting a passing officer. *Un drame à Séville* (*A Drama in Seville*) has Max challenged to a duel "in Spanish fashion" by a matador over a girl's affections. While he wins the girl for a time after being wounded, the matador strikes back in the end, according to its synopsis. *Kinematograph Weekly* remained very positive, concluding the latter film to be "undoubtedly one of the best of those issued this week, and [one which] should be seen."[45]

Early autumn 1907 resulted in few, if any new films, but November 6 saw release of *Les exploits d'un fou* (*Doings of a Maniac*), a sketch that seems to be about a "lunatic" escaping a mental asylum and causing havoc on the street. Mockery of the mentally ill was, of course, quite common (and presumably "accepted") in films and other entertainment of the day. Max appears to have played a smaller part of a passerby, though. Three days later, *L'armoire* (*A Cupboard*) hit the screens, with Max playing a womanizing husband, whose wife gets her revenge when he towards the end is "carted about on a moving van on a railroad train[,] and is unable to make his escape until he has had a nerve-racking experience."[46] Last out in the year was *Les plaisirs du soldat* (*Soldiers' Antics*), where he appears to have played a young aristocrat experiencing the hardships of military service.

More films were to come by the start of 1908, and so did work onstage. Although Max was getting well-seasoned on Pathé's timetable by now, he had not discarded Théâtre des Variétés altogether. On January 3, Alfred Capus' play, *Les deux ecoles*, premiered at the theater, with Max doing the smaller part of "Serquigny." On the same day, he also debuted as the star of the one-act play, *Passez, muscade!*, in the role of "Lucien Verdier." Both shows ran for over forty performances.

As if the New Year hadn't brought him sufficient exposure already, a day later, Pathé released two more brand-new one-reel comedies starring Max Linder: *Ma montre retarde* (*My Watch Is Slow*) and *Mon pantalon est décousu* (*In A Difficult Position*). While the former film is thought to be lost, the latter is available online today. Here, Max is once again cast in the role of a *boulevardier*, gracing the screen in an attire even more stylish than that of *Max Learns To Skate*. As he prepares himself for an evening out, he discovers the back of his pants is ripped. Being in a hurry, he sews the rip without taking the outfit off and rushes out. The patch job doesn't last long, of course, forcing him to spend the evening trying to hide his behind from public view, which ends in a predictably humiliating climax. Clocking in at 4 minutes, what makes this rather standard comedy work so well is Max's determination to maintain his dignity amidst the embarrassment. *Gentleman Max* is well underway.

Even so, his position at Pathé could not yet compete with that of André Deed, for sure. By all indications, Deed's character, Boireau, remained the company's hottest property for another while to come. Still unknown by name to movie audiences, it can furthermore be assumed that the heads of Théâter des Variétés were rather indifferent to Max's increasing success in films. He was not to be discouraged, however, striving onward in both fields throughout most of 1908, but then his engagements came to an unexpected halt, both at Pathé and Théâter des Variétés.

CHAPTER 7
MAX'S MURKY MALADY

One would think, perhaps, that Max by now was so established in films in the role of a well-dressed dandy that he no more would be asked to play the unruly youngsters of his very first films, yet *Le premier cigare d'un collégien* (*His First Cigar*) saw him return to that very role. For a long time assumed to have been made even earlier but probably released on January 11, 1908, this "sketch with a moral twist" has been one of his more readily available films. Directed by Gasnier, it follows a scenario often used (perhaps overused) in comic strips of the same era: depicting an innocent lad's first encounter with tobacco and its aftermath. Max is again dressed in school uniform, echoing his screen debut of 1905, but inevitably with more confidence in his performance. Preparing for an evening out, he slyly grabs a batch of his father's cigars and leaves home in good spirit. Once seated at a café, he self-assuredly lifts a roll to his mouth and lights it—only to soon find himself gravely nauseous. Back home, he is even unable to lock the door to his apartment at first, as he mistakes a cigar for his key. When he finally does get in, it turns out to be wrong apartment. While praised in one American ad as "[o]ne of the best comedies ever made,"[47] *His First Cigar* now stands as a rather typical half-reel comedy of the day.

The following month resulted in what must rank as one of the comedian's best films up to this time. Certainly excellent for 1908, and quite funny to this day, *Vive la vie de garçon* (*Troubles of a Grasswidower*) clocks in at 10 minutes, has thankfully survived in pristine condition, and is readily available for viewing. Here, Max and his wife both suffer an unhappy marriage. As the husband refuses to put down his paper at breakfast, the wife decides she's had it and leaves him, apparently for good. Max triumphantly celebrates, doing an impromptu dance and likely anticipating some treasured time alone. This, however, is the early twentieth century, folks, and the male soon finds himself not up to doing household chores after all. We follow Max as he tries to do the dishes (he winds up using a hose), shops groceries (he's robbed by an urchin), and helplessly prepares a dinner of sorts (while still in his top hat). As the next day escalates into supreme chaos and Max finally gets a whole closet over him (which cracks), he finds himself falling on his knees for forgiveness when the wife reappears after all.

Fun though the comedy still is, a couple of factors must've made it even more of a scream to audiences of its day. First of all, there's the temporary reversal of expectations with regards to the so-called *les rôles the sexes*, which are clearly of a different time. However, perhaps more easy to forget to a modern public, is how hard household chores truly tended to be back in the day. Making dinner and doing laundry *was* indeed hard work once upon a time, all the more so if you hadn't been taught how to do it, so Max's inaptitude makes perfect sense. It's the *additional touches*, such as his wearing a bloody *top hat* while dropping a hen in a pot, that makes it hilarious (as it no doubt did to viewers of 1908, as well). Max is growing all the more comfortable in front of the camera; his gestures look swift and effortless, and he often allows for small extra bits of comic business in his performance, as all the better silent comedians of later years were also apt to do.

Creative boost—and a disappointment

Max's work capacity seemed boundless at this time. By spring, he was approached yet again by Théâter des Variétés, this time to play "William Touret" in the four-act comedy, *Le Roi*. His friend, Max Dearly, also appeared in the play. Premiéring April 24, 1908, the staging proved a smash hit by Théâter des Variétés' standards. Max was singled out for his performance in press reviews; *Le Figaro* declared him "the most skillful of young ranters."[48]

Meanwhile, Pathé kept cranking out a steady string of Max Linder one-reelers. *La maîtresse de piano* (*The Music Teacher*) has him once again in drag, as he impersonates a female music teacher so he can visit his girlfriend without her skeptical father knowing it, a premise he would revisit years later in his feature, *Be My Wife* (1921), albeit without skirt. In *L'obsession de la belle-mère* (*Tormented By His Mother-In-Law*), he again mocks the obstacles of family life. Georg Renken notes that, upon this latter film's Brazilian release in June, Max Linder is actually mentioned by name in the daily *Jornal do Brazil*, describing him as the "popular and extraordinary comic Max Linder."[49] Brazil's awareness of his identity was no doubt of recent origin; the French magazine, *Comœdia*, had revealed his name for possibly the first time just three months prior, stating flatly that he "would gain a wordlwide popularity if his name appeared in the programs."[50] Such it was not to be, however... not yet. Excepting a few fortunates such as André Deed, *Pathé*'s name was still the heavyweight to be considered.

Yet Max's credits thrived. The lost film, *Deux grandes doulers* (*Two Great Griefs*) marked another temporary shift from comedy. Released July 17, 1908, here grieving widower Max acquaints a lady in the same somber situation as he, according to a synopsis. The rest of the year's filmography seems to have only dealt in comedy, however. As was customary in comic films of the time, most of the scenarios present Max struggling with a particular quandary which is instantly implied in a given film's title: in *Mes voisins font danser* (*Noisy Neighbors*), he's battling a headache; while in *Un jeune homme timide* (*A Shy Fellow*), he suffers from severe timidity. Save for a few titles mentioned earlier, little of his output from this year is readily available today. Still, it is evident that he underwent a creative boost in the first half of 1908.

Just for that reason, it likely came as quite a letdown when his career all of a sudden had to be interrupted. Renken notes that, on September 18, "Parisian newspapers" proclaimed Max to be "dying."[51] The cause was not given. "Initially," says Renken, "his condition improves and he can take up his role in *Le Roi* again, but after just over two weeks, he must be replaced by a colleague, for the following five months."[52] The actor replacing him was Albert Reusy, who had appeared in the play from the start in another role. Max remained absent from Théâter des Variétés between October 17 and March 10, 1909. In the meantime, Pathé appears to have cancelled, or at the very least not renewed his contract. In November, the company released *Les tribulations d'un neveu* (*Surprise Package*), a comic sketch with Max again playing the role of a school boy, the final effort of a prolific year, and, in fact, the last for months to come.

CHAPTER 8
MAX IS BACK ON TRACK

Even as he recovered from the unnamed illness which, at first, was feared to be fatal, Max seems to have been able to get some work done. According to an article in *Comœdia*, which Renken cites (admittedly published one and a half decade later), Max appeared briefly in the role of "Blond" in a staging of *Le Roi* that was held in his hometown Bordeaux for a few weeks in January 1909.[53]

As spring approached, he had become sufficiently well so that he could return to Théâter des Variétés for the rest of *Le Roi*'s second season. By June, the play had reached no less than 350 performances at the theater. By this time, he had also signed another contract with Pathé to work at the studio full-time. Although he was still to do some sporadic stage appearances in succeeding years, from this time on, *le cinéma* would remain his priority by far. The days of alternating between stage and screen were practically over. Movies, he had discovered, was a business to be taken seriously.

The first film to be released after his "comeback," *Un bobo mal placé* (*A Case of Lumbago*), hit the screens on June 22, 1909. Although lost today, a synopsis declares the sketch to be a "very amusing picture [which] shows a fellow who is suffering from a bad case of lumbago, and [so] the excruciating pains which shoot through his system at every move causes him to wince and turn into all sorts of grotesque shapes."[54] Viewers suffering from lumbago may not have found the comedy equally amusing, but Max's screen return appears to have been thoroughly well-received.

Back again—more than ever

Indeed, the comedian quickly found himself back on track. His first one-reeler of the year was followed up by *Aimé par sa bonne* (*Loved By His Servant*) in July, a film that received a very favorable review in the United States, calling it "a series of laughs all through, depend[ing] largely for its success on the admirable pantomime of a Pathé comedian whose face has been absent . . . for some months." It was also predicted that the return of said "Pathé comedian" would be "warmly welcomed by many admiring patrons of [the] picture houses."[55]

As indicated in the American review above, Max was by and large still unknown by name, but as autumn progressed, this was now finally to change, no doubt to the actor's great relief. André Deed's departure for Italy earlier in the same year had almost certainly played a role in this. Also, Pathé had likely become more willing to take a risk on Max's behalf, so to speak, now that he worked for them all days of the week. In the late months of 1909, his name began to pop up in film ads all over Europe. The earliest mention of the comedian in Norwegian press that the author has been able to find is dated October 5, 1909, in an ad for the film *Une conquête* (*A Conquest*, in Norwegian *En Erobring*). Max is proclaimed as "France's greatest humorist."[56] By spring 1910, his name was regularly listed in American papers, as well; an ad of May 4 describes *A Cure For Timidity* as "[o]ne of Max Linder's funniest comedies."[57]

By now, nothing implied that the comedian had been seriously ill just a year before. September 4, 1909 saw release of *Amoureux de la femme à barbe* (*In Love With The Bearded Woman*); September 24 brought *Un mariage américain* (*Miss Moneybags Wishes to Wed*) to the screens; while October 15 provided *Les surprises de l'amour* (*Love's Surprises*). The latter title was, no doubt, derived from Jean-Philippe Rameau's ballet, *Les surprises de l'amour*, and opens with Max faking a fever so that he may get excused from breakfast with his parents and brother. He subsequently escapes to visit his mistress. Both his father and brother repeat Max's play just a minute later, however, also to get away to a mistress, who, of course, turns out to be the same woman. In the end, all three conclude that the lady is not worth rivaling about. Papa Linder hands out a check to each boy to make sure that they'll keep quiet about the affair, and they all grin. *Finis*. A well-used scenario even at the time, this 6-minute film is perhaps most notable for its opening scene. As he's about to make his escape from home, Max gives a sly look to the camera, as if saying "now, just *watch* me as I fool these poor *saps* here." He's as eager to interact with "us" as his fellow actors, or as critic Walter Kerr later said of Chaplin, he almost *flirts* with us. Little wonder, then, that he by now had begun to conquer the hearts of his audience for real.

A Prince Arrives

Despite André Deed's exit on Pathé's lot, however, Max would not be totally without a rival in the ensuing months and years. During his temporary absence, yet another comic actor had risen to fame at the company. Born Charles Petitdemange-Seigneur, but widely known as Charles Prince, this up-and-coming comedian was, in fact, ten years Max's senior and a Vaudeville veteran by the time he made his first regular batch of one-reel films. Named "Rigadin" in his comic sketches, Prince's popular breakthrough occurred more or less simultaneously with that of Max. Thus, he is often described as Max's only serious competitor in the years before World War One. Although also frequently cast in the role of a dandy and exposed to mishaps akin to Max's, however, their differences were arguably more striking than their similarities. While contemporary audiences may not have seen it that way, at least today Prince appears rather unsubtle in his methods when set up against Max. Though the situations he finds himself in are often amusing, he comes off as much more of an obvious buffoon than Max. In that regard, his style is closer to André Deed's, in my opinion. (In fairness, the films with Prince which the author has been able to view have been from the early 1910s, and it is, of course, possible that he matured more as the years went by.)

Nonetheless, just like Max, Prince was to visit many themes and premises in his films that later comedians were to build upon—however broadly. In *Rigadin père nourricier* (1913), Rune Walderkranz notes, he adopts an abandoned child years before Chaplin's *The Kid* (1921) or Harry Langdon's *Three's A Crowd* (1928).

Keeping it up

It's unlikely that Max felt seriously threatened by Prince's increasing stature, though, as the proportions of his own acclaim were by now skyrocketing. At least nine more one-reelers saw release before year's end, all of them duly covered in French and foreign press. In *Petite rosse* (*The Little Vixen*, October 22), his eccentric fiancée gives him a curious ultimatum: lest he learns to juggle, she won't wed him. As the British *Bioscope* eloquently outlines in their review: "[w]ith his usual . . . unquenchable enthusiasm, the impetuous [Max] rushes home and soon wrecks his apartment with amateur legerdemain, but with no satisfactory results." Even so, after a while he surprisingly decides to write "a note to the fair damsel, declaring that at last he is in a position to claim her." As she arrives with her father, Max places himself behind a room divider and starts to juggle, displaying a great "agility with the balls." The girl is suspicious, however, and quickly "overturns the screen, and [thus] discloses a professional juggler, whose services the deceitful lover has enlisted to perform the difficult feat." Perhaps not among his most memorable efforts when viewed today—the ending is quite predictable—*Bioscope* nonetheless concluded that "[w]e need not dissert upon the [humor] of the subject, which is always assured when Mr. Linder is acting."[58]

In *Roméo se fait bandit* (*Romeo Turns Bandit*, November 19), Max's sweetheart is of a more agreeable type, but her father is unimpressed with our hero, refusing him to see her. As attempts to convince the old man lead nowhere, Max stages a devious plan: disguised as a bandit along with a couple of friends, he kidnaps the father and ties him to a tree, whereupon the "bandits" promise to kidnap the girl next and keep her for ransom.

An American reviewer summarizes: "Max now presents himself before the father [undisguised] and offers to rescue [the girl from the 'bandits'], accomplishing the feat with a droll show of bravery and prowess that wins the old gentleman's gratitude and the hand of his daughter."[59]

The available print of this film appears to be incomplete, unfortunately. There's only a hint of the scene with the "droll show of bravery and prowess" in the version I've seen, making the sketch's ending rather confusing to anyone without a synopsis at hand. In any case, Max was to return to the basic plot of this film in the feature, *Be My Wife* (1921), there pretending to be rescuing his sweetheart and her aunt from an imaginary burglar.

The release of Max's very last film of 1909 seems to have coincided with New Year's Eve. The by now lost film, *Les exploits du jeune Tartarin* (*The Adventures of Tartarin the Younger*) apparently portrayed him as "a youthful hunter who has just returned [home] from the wilds of Africa with astounding stories of his prowess" to tell, according to a synopsis.[60] However, as the hunter is visibly shaken by "a large and rather powerful individual who asks him for a match," as well as "a mouse in his bedroom," his listeners begin to wonder if his tales aren't just some fancy fiction.

The Bioscope concluded Max, once again, to be a comedian of "inimitable humor."[61]

A dismal winter of illness notwithstanding, by late 1909, Max had recaptured the screens of Europe and the United States, to a degree even more striking than before his hiatus.

Yet, his greatest triumphs still lay ahead.

CHAPTER 9
MAX MAKES DIRECTOR

His public approval now an indisputable fact, Max's farces were to generally extend in length somewhat toward the end of 1910, some of them clocking in at a quarter of an hour, but most of his misadventures were still wrapped up in just a few minutes. In his first film of the New Year, *La timidité guérie par le sérum* (*A Cure for Timidity*, January 14), he returned to the role of a henpecked husband (with a flinty mother-in-law back on the scene). The same month also saw release of the (now lost) sketches, *Une bonne pour monsieur, un domestique pour madame* (*Sevants and Masters*) and *Jeune fille romanesque* (*A Romantic Girl*); the latter, it was said, was "an especially well-acted farce in which the popular Pathe [sic] comedian . . . appears in a characteristic part,"[62] presumably as that of a man-about-town.

Louis Gasnier and Lucien Nonguet served as the comedian's regular directors by now, more or less, handling the majority of his films. However, it appears that Max had also begun to provide, with increasing frequency, scenarios of his own by this time.

A risqué scene

One film made this winter that survives in good shape is *Je voudais un enfant* (in UK *Max Linder's Big Family*). Directed by Gasnier and released in Denmark on February 18—apparently before its French release, even—this brief sketch enacts a story that one suspects was deemed too risqué in many countries, the United States included. Max and his wife are unhappily childless, their frustration seriously threatening the family peace. As he sits down to read the paper after another quarrel, however, he spots a promising ad; it turns out that a (predictably eccentric) doctor in town offers pregnancy assistance through a mysterious prescription. Their spirits suddenly aroused, the couple hurry down to give it a try, and, sure enough, back home Max is presented with an infant child, miraculously "produced" on the spot. Then comes another child—and another—and then plenty more. In the final shot, a despaired Max finds himself more or less bombarded with infants on the living room floor.

The less prudent portion of the public in 1910 no doubt found this final scene a blast, but as one watches *Je voudais un enfant* today, most viewers will be primarily concerned about the well-being of the crying infants in the film, as they're rather carelessly scattered about on the floor and clearly wondering what the heck's going on.

Winter marched onwards. Yet two new more screen sketches hit theatres on February 25, 1910: *Soldat par amour* (*The Orderly*) and *Le serment d'un Prince* (*A Prince of Worth*). Though one could have reasonably assumed that Max was cast opposite his rival, Charles Prince, in the latter film, he is actually the one to carry the royal title himself, as he briefly abandons his dandy character in favor of outright kingship. Interestingly, he seems to have temporarily resumed his much earlier pseudonym on this occasion, as he's given the name of Prince Lacerda in the film's intertitles.*

Olympian scenery

While Max's days at Théâter de l'Ambigu-Comique and Théâter des Variétés were definitely over—indeed, there is little to suggest that he ever again considered the stage a priority to the screen—he may have missed the intimacy of a live audience on occasion. At least he was to still accept a few stage engagements even as the new decade proceeded. As revealed by Renken, in April 1910, the comedian delighted audiences in *La Grande Revue* at the Olympia in Paris, as he entered the stage in an exclusive film entitled *Cocher! À l'Olympia*. In the sketch, Max was seen "hurrying from his house in a great state of excitement, fearing he [would] be late for the [theater]." As the film faded, however, Max suddenly appeared "in the flesh [onstage], tattered and torn after his adventurous trip...."[63]

Enjoying the glimmer of footlights yet again, Max would perform at the Olympia several more times in the months ahead. He did not allow the new work to interfere greatly with his obligations at Pathé, however (nor, presumably, did Pathé). If anything,

---

* This is made all the more clear in a Swedish print of the film, which is simply entitled *Prins De Lacerda* (Svenska Filminstitutet, Stockholm).

his return to the stage must have made him realize how far he had come by this point, owing to the flickering medium. By now, Max qualified as a bona fide superstar, very arguably the first of them all. Some may make the case for actress Florence Lawrence, who first attained wide-reaching fame as "The Biograph Girl" as early as 1908-1909; however, from what the author can see, Lawrence did not become known by her own name until the early 1910s.*

As Max trudged onto the Olympian scene, everyone in the audience was undoubtedly well aware who they had come to see. The two mediums had switched place, one might say; now it was rather the *stage* that provided a welcome additional paycheck.

Director Linder

It's odd that it didn't happen sooner, in a way, but as of *Max fait du ski* (*Max on Ski*, May 27) the dandy comedian's forename was to be included in his film titles on a regular basis, as had been accorded Deed's "Boireau" and Prince's "Rigadin" for quite some time. The Nonguet-directed *Max fait du ski* is today mostly amusing for its opening scene, as Max painstakingly fastens his feet to a couple of skis while still inside his apartment, resulting in quite a bit of struggle as he tries to exit his door. The rest of the sketch, which runs at barely four minutes, mostly consists of him stumbling up and down on the ski slope, finally crashing into a befuddled photographer in the snow.

In *Max est distrait* (*Max Is Absent Minded*, June 17), Max finally appears to have taken control behind the camera, by now feeling properly experienced to direct his own farces, though both Gasnier and Nonguet were still to step in throughout 1910. As likely the first of his regular directorial efforts, *Max est distrait* received mixed reactions in British and American press. *Moving Picture World* noted that "[w]hile the picture is mildly amusing it contains no startling novelty,"[64] while *The Nickelodeon* found it "a bit disgusting" that Max in the film "pours ... coffee into his silk hat and then drinks it"[65] (one hopes that this latter reviewer was spared from the many vomit- and urine-gags which frequented Pathé's

---

* As she worked at the Independent Moving Pictures Company (IMP), a widely-publicized fake death news item in early 1910 first revealed Florence Lawrence's real name to the public

comedies around this time). *Variety* went so far as to call the film "disappointing."⁶⁶

Of course, in those days screen comedies were still churned out with a density comparable to today's TV sitcoms, so an occasional bad apple meant next to nothing. Indeed, Pathé's trust in Max Linder as their major comedy asset would from now on be emphasized each time the question of contract renewal was brought up. In one American report of the year, he was said to have signed a deal granting him "a very high [annual] salary."⁶⁷ The exact amount is not verified, although Walderkranz claims 50,000F⁶⁸ (well over $300,000 today, as far as the author is able to estimate). In any case, his wage was doubtlessly to swell even more within just another year.

At this time, Pathé's farces still made use of plots so simple that they hardly qualified as plots at all, Max's included. Storylines were to increase in complexity somewhat within the next two to three years, especially as directors were afforded more length to develop their intrigues. However, in 1910 most film comedy still evolved around a single humorous predicament that was presented at the very beginning of each sketch and increased in scope toward the end. In *Trop aimée* (*Max Fears the Dogs*), for instance, we find him preparing to propose to his sweetheart, only to be interrupted by the woman's horde of dogs. Visibly scared of the canines, our hero proceeds to run—and run—and run—but the animals eagerly follow his tracks. Having broken into a baffled stranger's apartment and hurried onto the roof-top through a chimney, Max finally believes himself sheltered, but no; the dogs ascend the chimney, as well, surrounding our frightened friend only to affably lick him as they're all covered in soot, human and animal alike. Released September 2 1910, in this sketch, it's Max's stunned expression as the dogs embrace him in the last shot that's most likely to evoke chuckles today.

With *Les débuts de Max au cinématographe* (*Max's First Job*, October 1), Max spoofed his own cinematic debut of five years prior. By now an established star with half a decade's worth of screen experience behind him, the comedian had presumably acquired enough of a distance to his early struggles at Pathé to make fun of it all. As he enters the company's frontal office in the first scene—allowing for a brief cameo appearance by Charles Pathé himself—innocent Max believes he'll be treated as a star from the get-go. He is, in fact, hired, but only as a stuntman. Ordered to appear in a scene involving a family brawl, our poor "film star" is indifferently tossed out of a window, landing onto the asphalt below on his belly. A mattress is then thrown out *after* him, not before, along with lots of heavy furniture. In the final moments, Max is run down by a bicycle and mercilessly sprayed with a hose.

The basic plot of a young hopeful arriving at a film studio expecting to become a star only to be exposed to nothing but severe abuse was to be repeated endlessly throughout the silent era, and well into talkies, as well (see, for instance the 1932 *Doubling in the Quickies* with Lloyd Hamilton and Marjorie Beebe for a later example).

One American review of *Les débuts de Max au cinématographe* (admittedly written three years after its initial release) suggests that the mayhem in this film was regarded as a bit "old hat" also back in the day. However, the reviewer singles out Max to be "a relief [during] the exaggerated, hurried action" in the sketch.[69] For that matter, a Norwegian reviewer was rather ecstatic about the spoof, naming it "this season's absolutely funniest number."[70]

Bathtub play—and illness again . . . .

While some of Pathé's early films have aged better than others, there's no denying that these sketches quite consistently provide us with a peephole into a bygone era. In the Nonguet-directed *Max prend un bain* (*Max Takes a Bath*, October 22 1910), we get to witness a time when running water was far from commonplace inside city apartments. When Max invests in a bathtub for himself, he's obliged to fill the tub out in the stairway, using a public tap. As he tries to move the tub back into his apartment, however, he finds that the water's made it much too heavy. Our hero is not one to give up, though; he simply decides to take the bath out in the stairway, and keenly leaps into the water. Right then, he hears footsteps—rather inevitably, this being a stairway and all—and quite a scene erupts as some neighbors subsequently spot him (the fact that Max isn't nude, but wears a proper enough swimsuit, likely didn't make much difference in 1910). A cop is notified, but Max flatly refuses to leave his comfy tub, so the officer has no option but to carry the vessel all the way down to the police station with Max still inside it. He's duly brought before a judge, but makes a swift escape, racing down the street on all fours with the upturned bathtub shielding his back. As a crowd of furious officers chase him, he climbs up a house wall, with the bathtub still on him (!), reaching the rooftop, finally shoving the tub down again and onto the hapless cops.

Although Lucien Nonguet tended to rely more on action than subtlety in his films, *Max prend un bain* easily ranks as one of Max's funniest efforts up to this time, of all his early films that have survived. His facial expressions, coupled with some surprisingly fast pacing and ridiculous moments, such as him dragging the heavy tub on his back down the street, make for eight minutes of delightful silliness. A gorgeous print of this film is by now available on DVD. Granted, the stunning image quality arguably makes it a bit obvious that the "wall-climbing" at the end actually occurred on a painted carpet – nonetheless, this sketch remains good fun. Upon its initial release, at least one German reviewer found it to be "one of the most cheerful" films of that week's program.[71]

Unfortunately, all was not cheerful this particular autumn. Max's screen misadventures were soon to decrease in frequency once again and for several months to come. In November, the comedian suffered from appendicitis and had to be operated on immediately. While appendectomies were not quite as dangerous in 1910 as had been the case just a few years before, prolonged after-effects were still very common. He was reported to have been ordered to rest for nearly half a year afterward. According to Georg Renken, the illness seems to have coincided with a certain roller skating accident. Although this mishap is sometimes said to have occurred during a performance at Théâtre de la Cigale, Renken argues that it more likely happened at the Olympia in late 1910.[72] Indeed, Max later recalled that "[t]hey took me to [the] Olympia . . . into a number consisting of . . . boxing on skates. . . . This happened to me[:] one night I slipped and fell. . . . [and]

from the blow I was told of the peritonitis and had to have this terrible operation."[73]

Crucial though the surgical intervention was to his survival, there is no reason to doubt it was also a painful and debilitating ordeal.

CHAPTER 10
MAX BACK IN THE SACK

Tiring though his months of recovery doubtlessly were, audiences were not totally deprived of Max during his official absence, of course. For one thing, his popularity assured that his films were repeatedly reissued. Also Pathé had had a good chunk of un-released films on hand when the appendicitis hit him. Just a few days after his serious operation in November 1910, *Max cherche une fiancée* (*Max In Search Of A Sweetheart*) was released. Directed by Nonguet once again, this film has Max being smitten by two girls. At the onset, he delivers an identical love poem to each, with equal passion, and eagerly awaits their response. Both girls are more than willing, it turns out, until they compare notes and realize what's going on. They send a dog with a note to the infatuated Max, telling him to leap into a barrel whereby he'll get a reply, which he proceeds to do. The girls then attach a lock onto the cask and drop it off a cliff (woah, these damsels sure knew to take revenge!). As the barrel drifts off to sea with Max inside, he sends another note to the girls with the aid of a pigeon, saying that he'd rather search for some other girl instead.

An American reviewer didn't much care for the "barrel escapade," thinking it "a too violent departure from the action [in] the first part of the picture."[74] Certainly, *Max cherche une fiancée* is most notable today for Max's performance. He has definitely arrived at his vintage identity. While he does things in the film that, one would think, should have made him rather unlikable to us (wooing two girls and all), his innocently romantic attitude and general sweetness make us root for him all the same.

On New Year's Eve, the last Max sketch of 1910 hit the screens with Nonguet on hand as director once more. *Max ne se mariera pas* (*Max Is Stuck Up*) consists of a brief scene that hardly took more than a couple of days to shoot. Running at about three minutes, the film has been inaccurately but understandably thought to have been made at an even earlier point. Visiting the local baker,

Max's hands get entangled in a flypaper, whose glue refuses to let go as he heads for the home of his sweetheart, where she and her parents are expecting him for dinner. The meal proves most trying, however, as every piece of silverware and other objects get hopelessly stuck in his hands. The girl's father believes Max's erratic movements to be a sign of annoyance on the beau's part, resulting in an anticipated brawl. Again, it's largely Max's facial expressions that make this very simple sketch work so well.

Slow recovery

Whereas audiences of 1910 had come to expect a new Max Linder farce on a weekly or bi-weekly basis, the comedian's illness late in the year forced Pathé to more sporadically release the remaining titles that were made before his leave of absence.

It wasn't until February that the comedian's first film of 1911 was delivered to theaters. *Max a trouvé une fiancée* (*Max Is Forced To Work*) has him employing a storyline that Charlie Chaplin later was to make his own, in films such as *Caught in a Cabaret* (1914) and *The Rink* (1916), that of a young waiter impersonating a man of noble blood in order to win the heart of a girl. Of course, similar plots had no doubt swarmed Vaudeville stages for years prior, but even so, this farce on nobility remains quite funny to this day, displaying Max (at least seemingly) in top form as a comic. Reviewers thought likewise; one writer found the sketch to show "some very good comedy both in plot and action," causing "the laughs [to] come in rapid succession."[75]

Even by late winter, however, the real-life Max was in fact still unable to work. Six whole weeks passed before Pathé decided to leak out yet another of his unreleased films, *Max se marie*, which has him wanting to divorce the woman he's just married (causing the film, curiously, to be named *Max Gets Married* in the UK and *Max's Divorce* in the United States).

Then, another six weeks went by before *Max et sa belle-mère* (*Max and His Mother-in-Law*) saw release. This film has caused some confusion to historians in more recent times, because Max made another farce by the very same name a few years later. However, Renken maintains that the two films are distinct, referring to press synopses for corroboration. In this particular film,

Max appears to have made a plan with his servants to scare his visiting mother-in-law away from his and his wife's house.[76]

Family reunion—onscreen

As another spring unfolded, Max's health, thankfully, improved. Pathé clearly welcomed this, given that their stock of fresh films with the comedian by now was emptied, while the public demand for more "Max" persisted. The 10-minute long *Voisin, voisine* (*Neighbours* in the UK) was screened on July 28, directed by Max himself. Here, we find a girl planning to marry Max, when she finds a note suggesting that her fiancée is cheating on her. After much fury and distress, the two are finally reconciled, and Max promises to never look at another girl again (more or less).

Reviewers of *Voisin, voisine* tended to pay more attention to Max's return than the sketch itself. A British writer made no attempt to suppress his relief that Max was back in business: "This popular and ever-versatile comedian has been greatly missed from the pictures lately," he said, "owing to having met with a very severe accident whilst going through some of his marvelous performances before the camera-man.* . . . [However,] he pulled through and is now himself once again . . . taking his old place, which, by the way, has never been filled by anyone nearly so capable . . . ."[77]

Indeed, Max Linder had been sorely missed. It appears to have taken him some time to regain his previous strength, though; in the first few months following his revival, his films were released on a more or less monthly basis (as opposed to his previous schedule of two to three films a month).

His next effort is rather noteworthy, however, if mostly for its guest stars. Released August 25, *Max Linder en convalescence* (*Max is Convalescent*) includes his real-life parents, Jean and Suzanne Leuvielle, appearing as themselves, along with his sister, Marcelle, suggesting, perhaps, that the comedian's elders had finally come to accept their son's chosen trade of work. Shot outside the Leuvielle mansion amidst their idyllic garden, the opening scene shows Max lovingly embrace his family as he returns

---

* As noted above, however, Max's accident of late 1910 seems not to have taken place in front of the camera, but most likely while onstage at the Olympia.

home, supposedly, for a vacation. Running at over 10 minutes, the family reunion provides some rather cute scenes, with a climax echoing Hepworth's famous early film, *Rescued by Rover* (1905), as the Leuvielles' family dog bravely saves Max from drowning. While it cannot be said for certain that none of Pathé's other comedians—André Deed or Charles Prince—ever did a "family reunion" onscreen such as this, there is reason to believe that the premise wouldn't have worked nearly as well with them as it here does with Max. It's his determination to not have his character portrayed as a dumbbell, but rather as a relatively believable human being with a comic flavor, that makes room for the gentle moments in this film, including his rather touching arrival back home at the beginning. With a more exaggerated comedian, on the other hand, it would arguably have come off as out of character, or even plain odd.

Reviews of *Max Linder en convalescence* reveals that Max's reappearance was still not taken for granted by the end of the year and into the next; one American writer declared that "[w]hether or not the [family reunion] enacted in this picture [is] authentic, one still experiences a glow of genuine pleasure over the privilege of renewing the acquaintance [with] this prince of merrymakers..."[78]

The public's delight in the newest string of Max Linder films by the latter half of 1911 hardly lessened over their visible improvement in quality. This must partly be attributed to the many advancements made in the film industry in general, no doubt, but no less importantly, Max seems to have reached a new level of confidence both as a performer and director. As his daughter Maud later put it, "Until this point [c. 1911], Max's films were designed as amusing sketches, [whereas] he now would make ... short narratives."[79]

The next "narrative" out, *Max a un duel* (*Max Fight a Duel*), was released September 22, 1911, and is a particularly funny one. Here, Max is once again presented with a nutty ultimatum by a fiancée: lest he fights a duel, she says—*any* duel—no marriage between them will occur. Thus, the film is spent on Max trying to provoke poor passersby into fighting him. He finally succeeds and wins the ensuing duel, to his girlfriend's delight. However, when a bill reveals the fight to have been "staged," he remains without a wife after all. Directed by Max, the comedy was said by one reviewer to be "a scream from start to finish."[80]

More duels in sight

Max's subsequent misadventure also centered on duels, although this time not out of any desire to fight on his part. Released December 15 and based on a script by Maurice Delamarre, *Max victime du quinquina* (*Max Takes Tonics*) stands as one of his most famous (and very best) short films. It's a pity that the most accessible print of this sketch is rather worn, though better copies are rumored to exist. Running at 15 minutes, this story of Max's overindulgence in "tonics" does not only provide an out-and-out hilarious performance by him, but also presents a neatly structured comic plot: following an illness, Max is ordered by his doctor to take a glass of tonics with alcohol to each meal. As he's served a morbidly large,"Bordeaux" glass by his maid, however, our hero soon gets predictably drunk, whereupon he decides on a night out. Once outside, he finds himself offending one respectable gentleman after another, but being much too tipsy to give a whoop about it. They all challenge him to a duel, so Max ends up with a handful of visitor's cards in his pockets, one card of an ambassador, one of a diplomat, and one (lo and behold) of the chief of police himself. Several cops try to arrest our drunken friend, but they're all taken aback as he each time hands them one of "his" cards. Finally, he shows a cop the police chief's card, whereupon the cop, naturally, assumes Max to be his superior in person. Following an awkward salute, the puzzled officer dutifully escorts him "home" to the police chief's house, where he's quickly thrown out of the window. As he literally lands on the cops he's previously fooled, the officers finally realize they've been tricked and give our hero a heavy beating.

While *Max Takes Tonics* doesn't give the comedian much room to display the "sweetness" that his character tended to radiate in his better films—he's much too drunk for that here—it still serves as first-rate proof as to how superb a screen comedian he had become by this time. It's also worth to note that while Max is indeed on a bender throughout the film—not generally considered a "sympathetic" trait, perhaps—he is not entirely to blame for his drunkenness. After all, his maid does hand him a much weightier glass than he expected, as he's about to take his medicine. The fact that Max gets drunk not really out of a *desire* to get drunk, as many another screen clown might've done, makes the unlikable things he does in the film arguably less obnoxious to us, though no less droll, for that reason. Max clearly knows what he's doing here.

With *Max Takes Tonics*, *The New York Dramatic Mirror* was quite taken once again, calling the film a "well worked out" farce that offered "a good many laughs."[81] For the record, one highlight moment of the film occurs when Max's coat gets entangled in a lamppost, causing quite a struggle for our hero as he tries to get loose, by now a classic gag that Stan Laurel was to repeat in the two-reeler *Pie-Eyed* (1925), as well as many other comedians. Played alongside a fitting musical score, *Max Takes Tonics* remains a scream, as far as I'm concerned.

As 1911 closed, Max's yearly salary is reported to have reached 150,000F.[82] By now a plainly wealthy man, the comedian settled down in a "cozy little apartment" on the Quai d'Orsay,[83] located in the 7th arrondissement of Paris (not far from the Eiffel Tower). Pathé now regarded him a top priority at their studio, for sure, this despite André Deed's return to France earlier in the year.

CHAPTER 11
MAX MIXES WITH THE MASSES

By January 1912, Max had resumed his earlier, hectic-but-highly-prolific schedule. What's more, he had assumed the director's chair on a near-permanent basis. A few exceptions aside, he was to henceforth supervise the vast majority of his own films for the rest of his career.

The year took off with a pretty good effort. Released January 5, *Max lance la mode* (*Max Sets The Style*) may be said to provide a modernized take on the story of *The Emperor's New Clothes*. Max is once again about to get hitched, when the sole of one his shoes inappropriately comes off. Being in such a hurry, he has no option but to purchase the all too large shoes of a passerby and run off to the wedding, infuriating the father of his soon-to-be bride with his odd appearance. Never in lack of a solution, Max convinces the old man that large shoes is the new *in*-thing. Following the ceremony, then, an entire gathering is seen dancing in ridiculously oversized footwear, "which makes an amusing scene," as one American reviewer put it.[84]

Another fine short released this winter was *Max et son chien Dick* (*Max and His Dog*). First screened February 9, 1912, this sketch has Max's dog warning his master that his new wife is having an affair. Max's reaction upon discovering his spouse's unfaithfulness is worth to note for its subtlety: as Max enters their living room and sees the woman accompanied by a man on their couch, he's about to fly into a rage, but he restrains himself and instead gives the shameful couple a simple smile of pity, while ordering his dog to bring the lady's suitcase. The scenario ends on a rather sweet note, though, as we see Max and his animal companion share a nice meal while nurturing a genuine friendship together.

Not all of Max's screen hazards were warmly received, however. In particular, *Une nuit agitée* appears to have caused Pathé some distress. Released May 8, we here witness Max being repeatedly irked by a flea as he's trying to sleep. What presumably made this scene so testy to audiences of 1912, however, was the fact that Max's wife is seen sleeping right next to him in the same bed, her face intimately pointed toward the husband's pillow. That she finally leaves the room in disgust, as Max's urge to kill the bug causes him to throw a mug of water over the bed, likely didn't help. Though I've been unable to verify that this film was banned in some countries, as is sometimes claimed, it seems to be correct that it went unscreened both in Britain and the United States. It should be noted that this didn't mark the very first time a married couple was seen cuddled up in bed together onscreen, and the sketch did make it to French playhouses, at least. Still, it goes without saying that such blunt intimacy wasn't everyday fare in films of 1912.

Tour of Europe

While Max Linder's name had been well-known to the public for years by now, his fame was to attain yet another layer of renown as 1912 proceeded. Though he had occasionally received attention in the press outside of film ads at least as far back as 1909, it was from this time on that film journals began to crank out extensive profiles on the comedian. All of a sudden, he found that being funny onscreen was no longer sufficient to mute the public's appetite for him; from now on, he was expected to be available for interviews, as well. In particular, one event that year would result in widespread publicity, causing reporters to seek out the comedian more aggressively than before. On April 14, 1912, German press announced:

"... Max Linder [is] expected to go on a tour of Europe under brilliant conditions. His absence from Paris extends to three months, during which time he will receive the nice sum of 60,000F."[85]

The idea to have Max embark on a far-reaching tour was not as obvious in 1912 as it would seem to us today. An insane level of popularity notwithstanding, it wasn't really until the late 1910s and early 1920s that it became self-evident for movie stars to undertake such expeditions to greet crowds of fans firsthand. Max, on his part, was quite certainly unprepared for what awaited him. Considering that much later stars such as Laurel & Hardy claimed not to have realized the extent of their fame until a world tour in the 1930s made it palpable, Max could hardly be expected to have given all that much thought to his "stardom" at this point.

Completely oblivious to his reputation he was not, however. Well before his first tour took off in the early autumn, he signed a new contract with Pathé that granted him the colossal sum of 1 millionF over a three-year period, making him probably the highest-paid entertainer of his day at that time.[86] In order to afford the deal, Pathé had to have the cost of his films raised. (Renken notes that, while the successful outcome of his 1912 tour is sometimes cited as the rationale behind the luxurious contract, this appears to be incorrect.[87])

Nonetheless, some amount of surprise undoubtedly waved through his mind as he arrived in Barcelona, Spain in September 1912. On September 25, the following exciting news were revealed in Spanish press:

"The remarkable artist Max Linder . . . will shortly come to Barcelona, where his fans will prepare a grand welcome. . . . The newspaper called *El Mundo Cinematográfico* has organized a banquet to be held at the Hotel del Tibidabo to flatter the illustrious mime . . . The festival promises to be a real event, a tribute of sympathy dedicated to . . . Linder, who enjoys worldwide popularity . . . The anticipation produced in artistic circles by the arrival of Max Linder is extraordinary. Some companies of our first [movie] theaters have gone to Barcelona for the purpose of recruiting the popular artist to make [a] debut in Madrid. We would welcome if this news were confirmed, to applaud the great French actor."[88]

By then, Max had in fact already made a performance in the city at the Teatre Novedades. Also, on the evening of the 25th, a banquet was held in his honor at the El Tibidabo restaurant, "attended by many in Barcelona belonging to the class of cinematographers."[89]

Two days later, at the hotel Colón, a female reporter had an interview arranged with the celebrated actor. As Max entered the hall, where their conversation was to be held at 12 p.m., he struck the writer as "a kind of perfect Parisian, of distinguished manners, which [he] unfolds with great naturalness, really handsome

. . . with all the freshness of a well-preserved youth, no trace of defects of any kind, seriously sympathetic, [and] not paying attention to the curiosity that he is the subject of."

When the reporter described the "queue of a few thousand people" that would flock to the playhouses of Barcelona whenever a new Max Linder film saw release, the comedian confessed to "dislike to exhibit" himself. "In addition," he said, "the civil governor [of Barcelona] . . . [has] expressed his desire that I avoid, when possible, the occasions that [may] result in the public to agglomerate [during my stay]."

"Surely your trip to Spain has some artistic purpose that we cannot penetrate," the reporter suggested.

"Oh, Senorita!" Max exclaimed, "[m]y journey has no artistic purpose. I want to pay tribute of gratitude [to the public] . . . I am much indebted to Barcelona and Madrid."

The "Senorita" was not totally satisfied with this answer. Surely "there is something that compelled you to start your [tour of] Spain," she continued.

"I can't explain why," Max replied, "but I feel a great affection towards this nation . . . From here [I] will march to Madrid, then back to Paris, and from there make another trip to Berlin and Vienna."

For some reason, the comedian was "[n]ot really wanting to leave for America," however. He also let out that he had originally "wanted to compose . . . five films" in Barcelona, arguably contradicting his earlier claim that the trip had "no artistic purpose," but he doubted that this ambition would prove feasible in the end.

Wrapping up the obligatory queries related to Barcelona, the subject changed to his life and habits in general. He claimed to do "three or four films" per week for Pathé at this point—an exaggeration—whereupon he gave some passing insight to his work methods: "I conceive [the plot of a film] . . . and as I direct my colleagues, who assist me admirably . . . the matter develops as we execute it."

"[So] you create and develop on a whim," the reporter remarked.

Max agreed.

The lady suggested that he must inevitably "like especially . . . comic work."

The comedian gently disavowed. "No Senorita. I am passionate about [the] serious genre . . . I like everything excessively sentimental, but . . . [the public does] not let me devote myself to it . . ."

When asked which cinematic genre he tended to prefer, Max again admitted to be most "attracted to the dramatic genre, [in] which I find more merit . . ."[90]

It's not rare to find a comedian who claims to prefer drama to comedy, for sure. In an early interview, Charlie Chaplin reportedly stated that he had "always been ambitious to work in drama, and it certainly was the surprise of my life when I got away with the comedy stuff."[91] Harold Lloyd is also said to have expected, and wished, to become a dramatic actor early on in his career. One should perhaps be careful, then, not to over-analyze Max's apparent preference to gloom over glee. Nonetheless, it seems not unreasonable to assume that his declared attraction to the "excessively sentimental" may in part have been a symptom of a personality trait within him. If so, this aspect of his character was to grow only more explicit in the ensuing years.

The conversation eventually landed on what sort of women bachelor Max liked best. He admitted to prefer blue-eyed blondes, although he made sure to point out that he found the dark-haired females of Barcelona "very beautiful, very elegant," as well, whereupon he remarked that he'd never been interviewed by a female reporter before. Finally, he promised to return to Barcelona "next year."

In sum, the Seniorita found "Max" to be "a true artist, a cultured man and a perfect gentleman."[92]

A day later, Max attended an amateur bullfight in the city, arranged "on behalf of the poor of the neighborhood." *La Publiciad* reported: ". . . As expected, the place was filled . . . Occupying a seat in the box of the presidency [were] Mlle. Napierkowska, the remarkable dancer, Angelita Villar, the beautiful soprano, and the sisters Mari-Marina."

As it happened, the comedian had been convinced to participate in the bullfight himself. ". . . The appearance of Max Linder, heading the team, was received with a standing ovation. Max looked nice, wearing green and gold. During the fight of the first calf, which happened at the corral, against the will of its matador, Linder exchanged various smiles, drained fourteen reeds of chamomile and allowed to be [photographed] two hundred times.... When the second [bull] was released ... [with] big, fine, fat horns wide apart ... the ladies were horrified, [and] apparently kept their divine eyes away from the arena, but Max Linder ... gave two large cleansing jumps with the pole...."

A rather dramatic scene followed. Max defeated the bull at the end of second round, but by third round, he was made to withdraw from the arena, as the public feared that he'd fail. Then "Linder, from the presidency, greeted the audience warmly and they corresponded gallantly to the sympathetic actor."[93] While present-day readers may find his joining in the bullfight less admirable than did the Spanish press of 1912, his participation does at least bespeak his willingness to undertake tasks which likely defied his comfort zone, all for the sake of "artistic purposes." The fight was recorded on film, and came to good use some months later, when the comedian set out to make the short film, *Max toréador* (1913).

More cities—more receptions

By the start of October, Max arrived in Madrid to be given a similarly grand welcome. Once again, he had to prepare himself for an extensive chat with a reporter. Writer A. R. Bonnat opened his resulting article by asking readers, perhaps rhetorically, how the actor would likely be received at the Gran Teatro, where he was to appear "next Monday" (October 7). "Surely well," Bonnat reasoned, "because Max deserves it.... His presence in Madrid certainly is a hot topic. There will therefore be a need to meet and chat with him for a while." This reporter was also impressed with Max's elegant appearance; "[h]e has his striped trousers [on]," wrote Bonnat, "just like in the movies. The only difference we notice in him [compared to onscreen], is that his height is lower than in the movies" (Max is estimated to have reached 5 ft. 2 in. as an adult, or 1.57m).

"How was Spain?" Bonnat asked.

"Bad," snapped Max back.

Before he'd had a chance to elaborate on this, however, the reporter asked him to speak about "his first steps in the theater world."

"I wanted to be an actor," Max explained, "but Dad was opposed. My family has a good reputation . . . and he had other plans for me. When I expressed my absolute decision to be a comedian, Dad said 'I [will] only let you if you enter the [state theater of] Comédie Francaise.' Just imagine! I was very young then."

"How old are you now?"

"Twenty-nine years," said Linder.* "I was twenty then. I came out with the first prize of the Conservatory [Muncipal de Bordeaux] and [for a time] devoted myself to the famous actor Le Bargy to give me a few lessons.** Certainly we were master and disciple alternatively, because while he taught me diction, I taught him fencing."

Perhaps surprisingly, Max then recalled that Le Bargy had in fact advised him against becoming a comedian: "'My dear Max,'" he paraphrased, "'your temperament is not for comedy. . . . I think you would do well to devote yourself to the theaters of the Boulevard.'"

Once arriving at the studio of Pathé Frères, however, Max admitted to have "earned a salary I never thought possible." He recalled his first monthly pay to have been 5,000F (certainly hyperbole), which had swiftly increased until reaching the incredible 1 millionF contract that summer. After briefly recalling the accident he'd been victim of at the Olympia, he shared a few more hints as to his work habits: ". . . I think out [ideas] by myself and I plan [them] to myself. Sometimes I'm lying down and toying with an idea when I start to see clearly the matter [before me] . . . [I then] jump out of bed, wrap myself in a gown, and on the spot start to unfold the matter [further]. When I have finished [the plot], I have to start thinking about another." Modifying his earlier claim that he had to produce three to four films a week, he now professed to be making fifty films a year. "That is almost one a week," he

---

* He had, in fact, two months left before his 29th birthday at this point.
** *Charles le Bargy* (1858-1936), well-known French stage actor, who also appeared in a few silent films.

emphasized, adding: "I have hired six actors, cast them, explaining what to do ... Meanwhile, the operator works and everything goes smoothly."

Towards the end of his conversation with Bonnat, Max finally got a chance to elaborate on his mixed feelings of his visit to Barcelona. It turned out that the press had been rather disappointed in his performance at the Novedades, treating him "very badly," though "the public, to be fair, much applauded" him. When he expressed a fear that there might be "a certain mood" against him in Madrid, the reporter quickly dismissed this worry as "nonsense."[94]

That Monday, Max appeared at the Gran Teatro of Madrid, accompanied by Napierkowska. To the city's delight, he was scheduled to appear every subsequent night throughout the week, but on October 8, he was yet again victim of an accident onstage. He still managed to do an abbreviated version of his act the following night, but then a bad case of fever apparently intervened, forcing him to cancel his remaining appointments at the Teatro. A few days later, the comedian left Spain along with Napierkowska and a couple of other companions, arriving in Lisbon, Portugal on October 15, where he performed at the Theatro da Republica for a few days.[95]

After yet another month, on November 15, Max set sail for Vienna, performing for two weeks at Die Theater Ronacher. At the start of December, he arrived in Berlin, enjoying a huge success with a performance at the Wintergarten. Again according to Renken, his two-week engagement had to be "prolonged by another two weeks" due to public demand.[96] Emperor Wilhelm II seems to have attended and greatly enjoyed at least one of the comedian's performances. Predictably, several producers are said to have tried to lure Max away from Pathé in favor of German film companies, but to no avail.

As his German engagement ended in late December, 1912, Max returned to France and Pathé. He was by now enjoying the very pinnacle of his massive fame; the public had grown practically insatiable of his presence. Thus, when he entered French soil yet again, another tour would prove to be just around the corner—with even more astounding results.

CHAPTER 12
MAX MATURES ON TOURS

Despite his tour of three months, Max's global swarm of admirers was not kept without his screen escapades in the latter months of 1912. The comedian had made sure to produce a solid number of films for Pathé's prior to his departure.

One title of this season stands out in particular. Released October 18, 1912, *Le roman de Max* (*Affinity* in the UK) is often cited as a favorite among Max Linder's hundreds of films. Here, Max enters a lovely seashore hotel, renting a room next to a pretty woman. As evening arrives, the two of them place their shoes out in the hall for airing and nod a bashful goodnight. As they close their doors, however, a mysterious spell comes over their footwear. All of a sudden, *one male and one female shoe fall fervidly in love!* We see them "kiss" and dote throughout the nocturnal hours. Next morning, Max and the woman exchange another shy nod, wholly unaware of the fantastic scene that's taken place a few hours before. Once outside, however, Max's footwear suddenly comes to life again, leaving its master helpless as it spurts back to the female neighbor and her alluring shoe nearby. Though at first embarrassed—who wouldn't be?—Max soon gives the lady a passionate grin as they witness their love-struck footwear "kiss," and so the two humans also embrace each other and live happily forever after. *Finis.*

Sweet and romantic though the film is, the idea to have two anthropomorphic shoes fall in love and then let their respective masters do the same wasn't as original in 1912 as one might think. Pioneering animator Émile Cohl had supervised a strikingly similar scene as far back as 1909. His *Les chaussures matrimonial* follows a near-identical plot, and the animated sequence with the shoes kissing in the hall is too much alike in the two films for it to be a coincidence.

Just as Max's work would influence a generation of film comedians, so did he no doubt let himself be inspired by others on occasion. However, while the plot of *Le roman de Max* may not have been Max's brainchild, his take on the idea works no less smoothly for that reason. Indeed, the character of Max seems tailor-made for this premise. In Cohl's film, it's the scene of the kissing shoes that's the major point (and the animation is very well done, for sure); in Max's version we find ourselves perhaps most touched by Max and the woman's emerging relationship, crucial to the story though the shoes still are.

A less romantic, but also quite enjoyable film saw release on December 20, 1912. In *Max et la statue* (*Max and the Statue*), a series of mishaps cause a sleeping Max, dressed in a medieval suit of armor, to be mistaken for a genuine armor, and so he is unwittingly installed at an exhibition in a museum. Next morning, he is "stolen" by a couple of dimwitted burglars, who are naturally terrified to then witness the suit come abruptly "alive." The final shot of Max whimsically playing a guitar while still dressed in the heavy suit is quite priceless.

One thing that may strike modern viewers when presented with Max's Pathé films is how relatively sparse they are in the way of *gags*. "Relatively" is the pivotal word here, of course. Certainly, there are gags to be found in his farces, but compared to the best work of Chaplin, Keaton, and other later silent comedians, the visual punchlines in Max's films seem rather few and far between, and rarely do the gags beget the kind of ping-pong effect that we now tend to associate with slapstick comedy. While audiences of the time did not necessarily see it that way, Pathé's brand of comedy may now strike us as primarily *situational*; that is, provoking laughter mostly through the cumulative effect of an absurd scenario rather than any individual jokes. This perspective does not apply indiscriminately, of course, for there are plenty of hilarious moments in Max's films that work superbly on their own terms, regardless of the story at hand, but a good case could be made that the concept of aggressive "gagging" didn't really come about until Mack Sennett's fast-paced Keystone films emerged in Hollywood a few years later. For that matter, Max's films were not always *intended* to be laugh-out-loud comedies. Nearly as often, his scenarios were designed to display a sweet or amusing *tale*, of which the aforementioned *Le roman de Max* was a good example.

Nonetheless, Max's films did evince a heightened level of "gagging" from this time on. All in all, the years 1912-1914 must rank as his most consistent phase of excellence.

A second tour in the works—though not quite yet

If the decision to let Max embark on a European tour hadn't been entirely evident in early 1912, it certainly was by the onset of 1913. On February 27, *The Bioscope* noted that arrangements for a Russian tour had been made, though several months would pass before the comedian actually went there. It's not clear if the long wait was deliberate, or if Pathé demanded that he make a certain amount of films before they let him flee again, which would not have been unreasonable, perhaps, considering his by now gargantuan salary.

Even at home in France, however, his professional duties were no more restricted to his hours in front of the camera. By now, foreign as well as native press would pester him for interviews in his office, to which the comedian usually obliged. In April, 1913, the Argentinian journal *Caras y Caretas* sent out its Paris correspondent for some "intimate details." In the resulting conversation, Max largely repeated what he had said to Spanish reporters six months before, though with a few extra anecdotes to add. He claims to have been born in Bordeaux—most likely, he saw no reason to be specific with a South American reporter—and went on to describe himself as "neither worse nor better than average" as a kid.

"I studied at several schools," he recalled, "getting good grades, but I had to put up with a lot. I didn't like science or history ... only literature, which was closest to my dreams, interested me. I was especially happy if a textbook at the school contained a piece of comedy or drama." He continued: "Not only did I [then] memorize it, but I recited scenes in front of my classmates and teachers with so much passion that my classmates broke into applause. As I grew older my love for the theater grew ... and at sixteen I [had already] worked with several amateur companies[,] when I finally decided to talk with my father ... [who was] strongly opposed [to my ambitions] and thus I left the parental home and came to

Paris. Here I did quite badly [at first] ... My father refused to send me a cent because he tried to defer me from my aspirations."

While Max's memories of his early years tend to be inconsistent as far as the chronology is concerned, the essential message remained explicit: his parents, or his father in particular, had not wanted him to become what he became.

Perhaps of most interest here is his statement that he had recently set out to write a film "that will have [the length of] a thousand meters, a comedy in three acts ..." [about three reels, or 36-40 minutes]. He then reveals that he'll arrive in Budapest "in a few days," and also mentions a "contract to appear" in St. Petersburg. The last half of the interview mostly recalls his earlier trip to Barcelona and Madrid.[97]

Like his Russian engagement, Max's trip to Budapest was postponed until late autumn. While it's not impossible that he did go to Hungary twice during the year, Renken notes that there is no evidence to support this.[98] Max was not kept idle throughout the spring, however. As implied above, the average running time of his films was still expanding.

Max Linder pratique tous les sports (*The Compleat [sic] Sportsman* in the UK) hit the screens on April 26, 1913. At sixteen minutes, this scenario has Max responding to an ad by a wealthy woman seeking "an all [a]round sportsman husband."[99] Along with a small crowd of other eager males, Max then sets out to prove his worth in a number of sports. This particular film doesn't appear all that exciting today; some tighter editing would arguably have improved it. As always, though, it's important to remember that contemporary audiences may have seen it differently. At least one German reviewer found the film to stand out among several other comedies released that week.[100]

More notable is *Max toreador*, released in Barcelona on June 14. This 13-minute comedy utilizes the footage of Max's bullfight the previous autumn. Unfortunately, the amount of animal cruelty displayed in the film arguably hampers some of its comic impact when viewed today. Here, Max attends a bullfight (as an onlooker) and is made ecstatic by the dramatic sight (these first scenes are the hardest to stomach, as we get to see real bulls getting pierced to death). As he strolls back home, his newfound enthusiasm leads him to stage a series of impromptu "bullfights" on the street. Without cattle at hand, he is forced to make use of various substitutes. Grabbing a cloth, he challenges an unsuspecting bicyclist. Next, he steps into a railroad track as a heavy engine rushes towards him, bouncing back just in the nick of time (this very dangerous stunt was most likely performed by a stand-in, as his character has his back turned to the camera throughout the sequence). Arriving home, he even gets his butler in on the game, commanding him to take down a stuffed bull's head on the wall and "play cattle." These animal-free scenes easily constitute the funniest parts of the film when viewed today. A bit later, however, Max is persuaded to purchase a cow to "practice" on, and her calf also goes along (the two animals appear genuinely reluctant to participate in the play). The last scene has Max triumphing as a "professional" bullfighter, and it's here the scenes from Barcelona come in.

Max toréador was received with expected enthusiasm and tremendous success in Barcelona, and the film was a hit elsewhere, as well. The last scenes in the arena were said to create "roars of laughter."[101] Its dire animal treatment has made the film age less well than it otherwise would have, but as stated above, the bits without the animals remain quite amusing in their own right.

About a month later, *Les vacances de Max* (*Max's Vacation*) saw release. Another rather funny short of the season, this comedy has Max being invited to his uncle's house for a vacation. The uncle is unaware that his nephew is married, and obviously looks forward to spend some "bachelor time" with Max, but our hero's wife is less taken by the idea and persuades her husband to let her go along with him (in his suitcase, no less). The rest of the film has Max struggling to keep his wife out of his uncle's sight.

Serving as Max's leading lady in this film was a young Gaby Morlay, an actress who was to reach stardom in France with a series of short films in the late 1910s, and later on in features, such as *Le bonheur* (1935). Morlay is thought to have reappeared with Max on a few occasions, such as in the later film *Deux août 1914* (1916). Of her association with the comedian, she mainly recalled to have looked "so dreadfully ugly [onscreen] that I feared my career would be over in an instant."[102] Late in life, when interviewed by his daughter, she made sure to label Max as an "impenitent charmer."[103]

Full-length duel shortened

Max's most remarkable effort of the year, however, once again cast him amidst a farce of duels. On July 25, 1913, the hour-long feature, Le duel de Max (Max and His Rival), hit the screens. The film was by far the longest production the comedian had yet made— what's more, it was the longest film comedy most audiences of 1913 would have had the chance to see. While Mack Sennett's Tillie's Punctured Romance (1914) has been widely cited as the first major feature-length comedy, starring Charlie Chaplin, Mabel Normand, and Marie Dressler, Max's film beat Sennett's by well over a year. It may still not have been the very first feature-length comedy to be produced, but quite likely the first to cast a renowned star comedian who also served as the major creative force behind the film.

The film was not screened in its entirety in all countries, however, mostly due to copyright issues. In one scene, Max performs the by now widely famous *"mirror routine"*—a sketch having Max and another man placed at opposite ends of an empty mirror frame, while both mimic the other's gestures so painstakingly that it looks as though each man is seeing his own mirror image. Ridiculous though it may strike us today that anyone would claim to have copyrighted this gag, such was indeed the case back then. Renken reports that Max had first seen the routine performed by "The Schwarz Duo" during his stay in Berlin in December 1912, and was so taken by it that "he decided to include it" in his new film, ignoring the fact that the Schwarzs had already had the act registered for copyright.[104] It can be assumed that "The Schwarz Duo" had not invented the idea from scratch; variations on this gag had certainly appeared in Vaudeville and Burlesque for decades, if not centuries, though they may well have refined and perfected it in their way. In the end, Le duel de Max had to be trimmed down to a "mere" 45 minutes in several countries, France included, though it seems to have been allowed to play at full-length in Britain, the

Netherlands, Australia, and Brazil, Renken notes. (At any rate, a film comedy of 45 minutes was seen as no small feat at the time, either.) For the record, as far as the author can see, the shortened version was also the one to be screened in Norway, though I'm uncertain if this was due to the rights issues, or if Norwegian exhibitors simply preferred the briefer film.

Abridged or not, *Le duel de Max* was treated with several glowing reviews. It was declared "a scream from start to finish" by one writer,[105] while an ad in the Australian *Sunday Times* said that "[t]he press notices of this [film] describe it as 'Max Linder's masterpiece.'"[106] Yours truly has not seen the film, but the largely positive reactions in the press should imply that, at least, the feature stands as an honorable early effort.

Did Max envision *Le duel de Max* as a "stunt" of sorts? He must, at the very least, have been aware of the risks involved, both artistically (no one truly knew how to make an hour-long film comedy back then) and commercially (*certainly* no one knew if the public would care for such a thing). Even after the tremendous box office success of Sennett's *Tillie's Punctured Romance* a year later, for a long time afterward, feature-length slapstick would still be looked upon as a gamble not worth taking by most. A slapstick-farce may fare superbly with audiences for ten to twenty minutes, it was thought, but over sixty minutes would get tedious at best. This attitude was to finally change by the early 1920s, obviously.

Though Pathé had given Max the go-ahead on his ambitious feature in the spring, it had clearly not been anyone's intention to let this represent a permanent shift of any kind. Following the release of *Le duel de Max* and its inevitable promotion, the comedian returned to his ordinary schedule, which by now consisted of about two short films per month, on average. Although many of his films now qualified as two-reelers (15 to 24 minutes in length), he still regularly churned out briefer sketches, as well. *Le chapeau de Max* (*Max's Hat*) is one such "filler," released August 23, 1913. This 6-minute sketch has Max being forced to purchase a new top hat for himself four times in a row when his last one gets repeatedly crushed (in a shortened version of the film, it happens "only" three times). First, his "chapeau" gets flattened as he enters a cab;

next a man accidentally drops a loose door over him; then a cat tilts a flowerpot onto his head. After yet another mishap, our hero has the foresight to ask for his fifth hat to be packed in a box, and so he strolls home to his sweetheart and her parents with relief. However, as he carefully places his hat on the living room floor (bottom facing upwards), the family dog finds it appropriate to urinate in it! When his father-in-law drops by next and demands to try the headpiece on, a devastating (and pee-filled) finale imminently occurs. (The amount of scatological humor present in some of these French farces may astonish modern viewers. In most American film comedy of the period, such jokes would at best be hinted at.)

Filler or no filler, it's surprising how well the very simple *Le chapeau de Max* works, and how amusing it still is. As so often before, Max's performance is largely responsible for this, probably more so than the film's incidents as such. In the first shot, he's presented to us as he gets ready for a promenade in the sun, unknowing of the mishaps that will soon haunt him. Dressed in his trademark attire, he does a graceful spontaneous dance before the camera, briefly scrutinizing his own appearance whereby he grins with childlike satisfaction. It's in snippets such as this opening scene, arguably, that Max's appeal is most striking. One understands very well why the public found him so enchanting in the first place. In addition to a striking pantomimic talent and attention to detail in his acting, he tends to carry a pronounced *enthusiasm* about him as he performs. He is very charming, simply put, which indeed must have hit his audiences as quite infectious. As always, of course, some amount of historical context is also recommended. Keep in mind that moviegoers of the early 1910s were ideally served a new Max Linder farce two to three times a month; he was a regular caller in their lives. As such, they came to "know" him in a sense— no doubt laughing before he had a chance to do anything funny yet—which cannot be fully duplicated today. Even the author, though having spent a fair amount of time repeatedly watching his work, must concede to this. Be that as it may, the charm of Max's little dance in *Le chapeau de Max* remains no less intact for that reason.

In another short film released in autumn 1913, Max aimed less for the big laughs. Released in Luxembourg on September 13, *Max fait de la photo* (*Max Takes a Photo*) appears to be a fairly straightforward, light drama. A case could be made that it's supposed to be parody, perhaps, but if so, Max sure didn't strive to make it explicit to us. Here we find Max eager to try out a new camera, when he bumps into a girlfriend on the beach, and he persuades her to let him take snapshots of her as she enters the ocean. Having posed for several photos in the waves, the woman finally goes ashore to a greenroom nearby. Max doesn't realize this, however, and believes her to have drowned. A desperate scene ensues. Our hero tears his hair and cries as a rescue team is alarmed to no avail. Finally, the misunderstanding is resolved, of course, and Max embraces his girlfriend with staggering relief.

There are a few comic moments in here, of course, but the only thing that truly suggests *Max fait de la photo* to be a comedy in any way is the fact that the *audience* is never led to think that the girl is injured. We know his despair to be groundless all along. Yet, the desperate scene is enacted with sufficient realism so that it's hard to find it comic. Indeed, Max's filmography includes several more such shots at light drama. Most likely, he saw the need for a *change of pace* on occasion, like any comedian, though he may also have welcomed the opportunity to showcase his dramatic abilities, as well.

Alhambra accident—and another tour

By late August, Max debuted in a month-long engagement at the Alhambra Music Hall in Paris, performing a slight reworking of his Wintergarten act from the previous December. His co-stars were Georges Gorby and British actress Hilda May. Once again, bad luck would intervene. On the fourth night, Max was victim of another accident onstage, when he lowered himself from a rope. Renken notes that the show was cancelled for the next two nights, but when resumed on September 5, Max had made sure to hire a stuntman for the risky sequences.

The prospect of another world tour had not been shelved, however. Whatever had delayed it, on November 14, 1913, Max was presented to a cheering crowd in Budapest at the Royal-

Orfeum. He appeared there nearly every night for the next two weeks.

During the engagement, German press reported: "The well-known film lion Max Linder . . . is playing a personal guest performance in Budapest. The pampered Parisian is quite well with us; he finds only one thing [disappointing] in Budapest . . . [a thing which] one would have expected him to [find] the least lamentable: 'Je n'ai pas trouvé une femme sérieus!' (I have not found a serious woman [here] yet), he said regretfully to our employee."

The article goes on to recount a troubling battle that Max apparently had had to endure following his Austrian visit the previous year: while in Vienna in late 1912, an impresario was said to have made the comedian sign an agreement for a three-day performance "for a provincial town." However, as the pay had not been outstanding, Max finally ditched the job. When the offended impresario learned of the comedian's current visit to Budapest in 1913, he proceeded to go to court, the article states, but Max refused to pay him back. In the wee hours of November 19, while asleep in his suite at the Ritz Hotel of Budapest, three strangers entered his room and robbed him of several personal possessions, including some valuable jewels. The unexpected "guests" had seemingly been sent out by the Austrian impresario.

However, this report above appears to have mixed the facts, according to Renken. Referring to an article published a year before in the German magazine, *Neues Wiener Journal*, this is what seems to have actually happened: Max had made a contract to appear at the London Hippodrome in early 1912. When his trip to Barcelona was arranged later that spring, he declined to fulfill his London engagement. As he arrived in Vienna in November 1912, an agent from the Hippodrome—*not*, as assumed, an "Austrian impresario"—sued him. The comedian was sentenced to pay a fine of "1,000 Kronen," which he ignored. The part with the three intruders at the Budapest hotel seems to be correct, but again, the strangers must have been hired by the London agent, not an "impresario" (unless the agent also happened to be an impresario, of course).[107]

It's unclear to this day how the matter ended. The French Consulate refused to get involved in the case, as they feared the bad publicity would cause tensions between France and Austria-Hungary (which may have been reasonable, since Max had been sued in Vienna, after all, though the conflict was about a cancelled London engagement). The comedian was advised to pay the "impresario," or, rather, the agent, back, but this proved difficult as "[p]oor Max Linder ha[d] no idea who robbed him in the name of the law."[108]

Despite this agonizing incident, his second world tour did, by all accounts, constitute a tremendous triumph. When he arrived at the central station of St. Petersburg on December 3, the crowd went near-berserk in their enthusiasm. Thousands of fans were about to literally "crush the fragile star," Walderkranz notes. "As had happened to Sarah Bernhardt during her visit, [the crowd] forced itself toward [Linder's] wagon and carried him triumphantly to his hotel."[109] As in Budapest, his engagement in St. Petersburg also lasted for two weeks. Apparently, a certain young composer named Dimitri Tiomkin (1894-1979) accompanied the act.*

With one arguable exception noted below, the rest of Russia proved equally infatuated with Max. A similarly rhapsodic crowd greeted the star upon his arrival in Moscow on December 16, his thirtieth birthday. While there, he performed at a cabaret known as The Bat, and on the first night found himself being received by a Max Linder lookalike (actually a makeup artist of the Moscow Art Theatre).[110] Next, he drove on to Kiev, a trip that resulted in a temporary letdown, as his engagement there had to be cancelled "due to a lack of spectators" (the reason, no doubt, being the high ticket prices rather than any lack of interest).[111]

Although the most celebrated star of a thoroughly "modern" medium, however, some of the looming Art Movements of the day were less taken by Max's frolics. Richard Abel notes that his Rus-

* Later a celebrated film composer, Tiomkin is perhaps best-known today for his Western scores for *Duel in the Sun* (1946), *Red River* (1948), and his Academy Award-winning Best Original Scores for *High Noon* (1952), *The High and the Mighty* (1954), and *The Old Man and the Sea* (1958), as well as his memorable score for James Dean's final film, *Giant* (1956).

sian visit was "frowned on by Russian Futurist poets, who feared it might prompt the press to make some undesirable parallels" between themselves and the comedian."[112] Abel quotes Futurist poet Benedikt Livshits (1887-1939), who in his memoirs lamented that Max's arrival had overshadowed a Futurist event held at the Troitski theater the previous day.[113]

At any rate, the comedian's disappointment in Kiev was more than compensated for by his ovation in Odessa, Ukraine on New Year's Eve, with Max "welcomed in the streets with hurrah and virtually carried on shoulders." His arrival caused "even the traffic [to be] jammed, which prompted the police to intervene."[114]

Last destination on the tour was Warsaw, where he was to stay for a two-night performance, inevitably sold out long before his arrival. This time, however, the comedian's welcome was disrupted by a personal grudge between impresario Moses Towbin and producer Aleksander Hertz, if a Norwegian press piece of two decades later is to be believed. Serving as Max's representative at the Warsaw Filharmonia, Hertz had eagerly awaited the star's coming, but it took longer than expected. Scheming to blackmail Hertz, impresario Towbin had boarded Max's train and presented himself to the star as Hertz in person (or Hertz's brother, by other accounts). As the train approached Warsaw, the imposter told Max to get off at a freight stop—pretending that they had reached the city—leaving the comedian befuddled as he entered what must have seemed a very pitiful central station. Towbin thought up an explanation and called for a taxi, which carried Max to the Hotel Polonia, where the impresario had booked a room. The report elaborated: "As this went on, a huge crowd awaited the comedian at the [Warsaw] central station, where a committee was present to greet the artist, while pretty girls prepared to endow their adored film idol with large flower bouquets. To the great disappointment of everyone, however, Max Linder turned out not to be with the train, and as disappointed spectators slowly left, the real Her[t]z tore his hair in despair. [Linder's] performance, which was to be held the same evening, had to be cancelled . . . ."

Finally, it was said, Hertz received a call from Towbin, demanding the sum of "6,000 rubles" for information on Max's whereabouts. The furious Hertz had no option but to pay up, whereby Towbin presumably fled to Berlin, while an "unsuspecting Max Linder was brought from Hotel Polonia to the theater, to at last receive the tribute of which he had been deprived upon his arrival."[115]

By the middle of January 1914, the superstar headed back for home once again, more assured of his wide-ranging adoration than ever before. Although the silver screen by now embodied a fair share of celebrity, including Mary Pickford and John Bunny in the United States, among comedians, Max Linder's stature still outranked that of practically anyone else.

His popularity would remain solid for still a few more months to come.

CHAPTER 13
MAX AND WAR FUROR

As on his first tour, Pathé had made sure beforehand that Max's fetching face remained a constant in the lives of "everyone" in the latter months of 1913, even though one didn't happen to live on the destinations where he had been scheduled to appear in person. Another solid bunch of one- and (to a smaller degree) two-reelers saw release while he was away, with one effort being especially noteworthy. Released December 20, 1913, *L'anglais tel que Max le parle* (*Max And The Daughter Of Albion*) evokes a warmth and charm that is arguably outstanding even by Max's standards: we see him entering a first-class train carriage headed for Paris, where he finds a pretty woman sitting by herself. The two are instantly taken by each other (of course!), but struggle for a bit to communicate—him being French, after all, and her being English. Max quickly solves the problem by fetching out a sketchbook and a pencil he has on him. As he doodles a (fairly simple) train, she grabs the book and outlines the Eiffel Tower. Next he does a sketch of himself (in top hat) "handing a bouquet" to the girl. She's in a cunning mood, however, and responds by adding a watering can above Max's self-portrait, so it "drenches" the drawn flowers. Seemingly offended, Max snatches the paper and slightly tears it, only to make it reappear as a "heart." As their faces split into a mutual grin, Max dares to give her a tiny kiss. Exiting their carriage, it's clear they've become a couple.

It turns out that the woman has gone to Paris to work in her father's new business, a store for bathroom facilities, and so the next day, Max decides to give her a visit (allowing for a nice shot as he passes the Eiffel Tower on his way, sporting top hat and all). Although at first delighted, the girl gets panic-stricken, as her father suddenly arrives with a costumer, making her shove Max behind the curtain of a portable shower. Inevitably, at that moment, the costumer wants to have the shower demonstrated, and so our top-hatted Max gets soaked in the last shot.

The final moments in *L'anglais tel que Max le parle* are standard farce, for sure, but the interplay between Max and the foreign lady in the prior sequence remains pure gold in its simplicity, a thoroughly sweet scene to this day. "What a delightful comedian Linder is," a British reviewer vouched upon the film's reissue several years later.[116]

Leading ladies

Notably, *Cécile Guyon's* role as Max's love interest in the aforementioned film actually gives her a chance to shine for a bit, whereas in general, Max's leading ladies tended to be rather anonymous unless a particular scenario demanded otherwise. This, of course, was in full accordance with the norm of the day; a male comic's female sidekick could be hired and discharged more or less on a whim. For her part, Guyon seems to have appeared in few other films with Max, though she was quite an active screen actress for a while, mostly doing dramas. Even so, many of Max's *femmes* reappeared with him several times. Lucy d'Orbel played opposite him in at least seventeen shorts between 1910 and 1915. She seems not to have done much other screen work, at least not that is known. Gabrielle Lange also did a good chunk of films with the comedian in the early 1910s—according to a French newspaper note cited by Renken, sadly Lange died at a young age in the spring of 1914, following "a long and serious illness."[117] Lilian Greuze also appeared in a good handful of Max's films throughout the year, usually billed as "Lili."

A New Year, a new era

The year 1914 has come to represent a time of great transition to historians, and no doubt for good reasons, although it can be assumed that the common man of the period largely plodded through his daily chores as he had done the year before. Amidst the emergence of atonal music, private dishwashers, and Marcel Duchamp's *Bottle Rack*, the pranks of Max Linder remained a dependable pastime to countless of households. He had become an institution, as the saying goes, his antics now slightly taken for granted by critics. As it turned out, his position as the indisputable King of Laughs would find itself threatened by year's end, but in January, he still very much reigned on the silver screens.

January 31 brought *Max pédicure* (*Max as a Chiropodist*) to theaters, presumably a remake of his 1908 film, *Pédicure par amour*. Here, Max comes to a woman's rescue, when her dog is kidnapped by a couple of urchins in the park. Expecting romance in return, our top-hatted hero follows her home, but is mischievously rejected at the door. This doesn't discourage him, though, and the next day he shows up outside her apartment again while she's having her feet tended to by a foot doctor. The doctor happens to be in another room with the maid upon Max's arrival, giving our hero full opportunity to charm the woman. However, her husband predictably appears in the hall that very moment. As the woman flees to another room, Max is forced to present himself as the foot doctor to the husband. The unknowing spouse figures he might as well get his own toes freshened up, and so, Max finds himself struggling to cleanse the man's well-trodden feet. Although the scene arguably runs for a bit long when viewed today, imposter Max's large-eyed frowns remain a merry sight.

In the spring, *Max et la doctoresse* (*Max and the Lady Doctor*) hit the screens. Presumably a remake of 1907's *Le mari de la doctoresse*, Max here weds a "lady doctor." As they find themselves man and wife, however, "each time he starts to embrace [her] she is called away to treat a sudden patient." Max finally "kicks all the patients out of [her] office and domesticity reigns supreme."[118] If one can forgive the film's core premise, which of course has not aged well (with the wife expected to just give up her career like that, contrary to her own wishes), it's an aesthetically well-crafted film comedy for its time. For the record, Max's apparent tendency in this period to do "remakes" of previous films does not necessarily signify any lack of inspiration on his part. As the medium of film had experienced quite an evolution since he started out nine years before, it seems only natural that he wished to rework and improve some of his earlier scenarios.

In *Max joue le drame* (*Max Plays Drama*), he again flirted with meta humor: released June 6, 1914, Max is here convinced of his abilities as a dramatic actor, and invites his less enthusiastic friends to a performance he is to hold in an amateur production. Lots of problems arise with the stage props during his delivery, however, making for a "really farcical" effect, as one reviewer put it.[119] One wonders if Max didn't exhibit at least a trace of self-irony with this film, considering that he had once been ambitious to become a dramatic actor in real life. In any event, though the sketch's ending with Max spraying the audience with a hose may appear a tad predictable by now, *Max joue le drame* still offers some amusing moments, for sure. The most memorable part may in fact occur at the very beginning, when Max gives a "dramatic performance" to his friends in private. Although slightly exaggerated for humorous effect, the scene nicely demonstrates his facial agility.

Five weeks on, *Max à Monaco* (*Max on the Briny*) hit theaters, featuring Max as he causes havoc aboard a yacht in drunken condition. A rather meandering effort (at one point it's revealed to Max through a pair of binoculars that his girlfriend is having an affair, but this is quickly all but forgotten), this drunken act is perhaps most interesting for how it, like the earlier *Max Takes Tonics*, strives to "justify" his clownish impulses in the film. Unlike many another, more exaggerated screen comedian of the time, gentleman Max would hardly have behaved as unruly as he does here if he didn't happen to be thoroughly intoxicated at the time. Meandering or not, *Max à Monaco* was praised in American press as "[a]n exceedingly funny comedy."[120]

Max's next adventure, *Max asthmatique* (*Max's Marvellous Cure* in the UK), has sometimes been confused with 1910's *Max fait du ski*, wrongly but understandably so, as this film also presents Max embarking on a skiing trip. Nonetheless, *Max ashtmatique* is more imaginative, for sure. Released August 28, 1914, Max is here instructed by his doctor to go on a vacation to the Swiss mountains. Our hero eagerly sets off a hillside with skis beneath him. However, the ride takes an unexpected turn as he never reaches the bottom of the hill, but instead ascends from the ground and finds himself sailing over the mountains, over cities, and over oceans. In the final shot, of course, we find our hero being awakened as he stumbles out of bed in his pajamas. More of a brief fantasy than farce, there is, in particular, a very appealing "dreamlike" quality about this film, made all the more engaging by Max's whimsical attitude.

Soldat Max

By the time *Max asthmatique* was brought to theaters, a crucial historical event had taken place. France was at war – with a substantial portion of Europe, no less. The incidents leading up to World War I have been meticulously covered by historians through the years, to say the least, and need not be repeated here at length. Following the assassination of Archduke Franz Ferdinand of Austria-Hungary by Yugoslav nationalist Gavrilo Princip in Bosnia's capital, Austria-Hungary had declared war on Serbia on July 28. By then, Russia had already begun to mobilize, prompting Germany to declare war on the Czar's empire a few days later. As Germany shocked the entire continent by invading the neutral (and mostly unprepared) Belgium, Britain declared war on Germany, and France soon followed.

Although the War's outbreak largely struck Europe like a bombshell, relations between certain nations had, of course, been tense for decades (if not centuries) by 1914. Generations of mutual mistrust had rumbled between France and Germany, and little suggested that the two powers would kiss and make up anytime soon, no more so after Germany's victory in the Franco-Prussian War. If the German popularity of Max Linder had served a soothing function between the two enemies, this now came to an end, as the War made the dispatch of his films across the border to Germany impossible. Furthermore, the comedian had enlisted for army service in August immediately upon France's participation. Apparently declared too fragile of stature for combat duty, after several more attempts, he was finally allowed to serve as a dispatch driver, Maud notes.[121]

Following the release of *Max et sa belle-mère* (*Max and His Mother-in-Law*) on August 31, two months went by before the public was granted a new Max film. More importantly, a most alarming headline appeared on Friday, September 25, in a Norwegian paper and hundreds of other papers across the globe:

"MAX LINDER DEAD?

"The well-known French revue- and film actor Max Linder is said to have fallen in the last great battle."[122]

Incidentally, on the same day, another paper announced the Norwegian première of *Et hastverksbryllup*, a new Max Linder farce, at Verdensteatret in Norway's capital city. *Et hastverksbryllup* was almost certainly the two-reeler, *Mariage forcé* (*Max's Chosen Bride*), which had been released in France three months prior. The ad proclaimed the film to be an "excellent comedy wherein one comic moment supersedes the next," having "the public in constant stitches."[123] It is a plausible guess that the fresh report of Max's assumed death put a hamper on the atmosphere at the playhouse that day.

Fortunately, Max wasn't dead, as it turned out, though nearly two weeks would pass before the world at large knew it. As late as October 1, *Washington Post* repeated the disheartening report, elaborating in a "special cable" to the paper:

> "Rome, Sept. 30. The death in the fighting in the battle of the Aisne of the 'movie' artist, Max Linder, is reported in a dispatch from Berlin.
>
> "Max Linder, 'the man with the $70,000 face,' was the moving picture hero of all Europe, and on this side of the water there are tens of thousands of 'movie fans' who will read of his death with a sense of personal loss. Perhaps no actor of the legitimate stage ever achieved such international fame and so great a following as this versatile man, whose voice was never heard by his audiences, but whose remarkably mobile features told stories from screens all the way from Petrograd to Yokohama...."[124]

Finally, after yet another week, millions of movie patrons were relieved to be told that the comedian was "only wounded," as reported in *The New York Dramatic Mirror*:

"For a week, the world thought that Max Linder, the famous Pathé star, had been lost to the screen forever, several cables from Paris telling of his being killed in battle at the front. But on Sunday the most famous comedian on the screen rose up in his wrath and denied that he was dead. The cable from Paris tells it this way: 'Max Linder telephoned from the military hospital at the front today saying that he was not even ill, but only convalescent, and soon will return to the service . . . .'"[125]

This reasonably uplifting report seems not to have reached all papers at the same time, however. Throughout the next two years, rumors of Max's death would resurface in Norwegian press from time to time (and no doubt in other countries, as well), until he was at last firmly stated to be "alive" in 1917.[126] For that matter, "the man with the $70,000 face" wasn't in quite as sound a condition as this last American article gave the impression of. In a later interview, Max revealed that he had in fact been physically harmed during his service, though he didn't go into details on that occasion.[127] (2020s update: Lisa Stein Haven has done much research on Max's war stories in her 2021 biography and debunked rumors.)

A few weeks after his return to the front in November, he seems at least to have been victim of a car accident that could have ended fatally. An American journal later reported that the comedian had been "driving at terrific speed, without lights, [whereupon] a collision [had] occurred. Max was violently thrown out and badly injured."[128] Max also recalled in a later interview that he, at one point, had been forced to seek refuge from a German patrol in icy water beneath a bridge for several hours, apparently resulting in a serious case of pneumonia.

In the end, Max found himself discharged from the army by early March 1915, after six months of service.

In-law troubles—once again

Audiences were not kept totally in lack of Max's mishaps during his months of service, of course. Just as during his world tours of the past two years, Pathé had sat on a decent pile of his films that were yet to be released as he entered the army in September.

The aforementioned *Max et sa belle-mère* is a rather well-known farce of this period. Running at two reels, we here find Max once again being henpecked by a domineering mother-in-law. As he and his wife prepare for their honeymoon in the mountains, the old woman insists on going along, much to Max's frustration. As the three of them set out on a skiing trip, our hero's temper finally reaches its limit, and so he pushes the hapless *belle-mère* down a slope. In the end, of course, the little family is reconciled, and all is forgiven and forgotten. Clocking in at nearly half an hour, the film arguably feels a bit long when viewed today, and the scenes with Max losing his temper over the aging in-law are apt to make a modern viewer somewhat uncomfortable. It was well-received upon its release, however, one writer declaring it "one of the funniest offerings of this nature that we have ever seen."[129] For the record, the scenes in the mountains, which constitute the vast majority of the film, appear to have been shot around the Chamonix Mountains of Switzerland.

While *Max et sa belle-mère* may not have aged quite as well as some of his other films, plenty of his two-reel comedies of this season demonstrate a deftness in their execution quite remarkable for the time. The two-reeler *Max au convent* (*Max's Elopement*) stands as perhaps one of his best works of the year. Released in November, 1914, this story has Max's sweetheart being sent by her father to a convent school, as the parent doesn't approve of her relationship with our hero. Max soon shows up at the school regardless, of course, determined to save his beloved, resulting in quite a funny scene as he finds himself being chased by a horde of furious nuns. There's also a nicely-choreographed scene prior to his arrival, featuring the white-clothed nuns doing an unexpected "dance" with identical movements in the school hall.

When Max's last film of 1914 hit the screens as *Coiffeur par amour* (*Max the Hairdresser*) a day before New Year's Eve, his comic adventures still remained very much a regularity to millions worldwide, even as his films now suffered a more limited international distribution as a result of the war. Two weeks before, the comedian had had the Parisian cinema Pathé Journal, which he'd managed since a year prior, renamed as Ciné Max Linder.*

Little could anyone have foreseen at the time that his level of output was soon to become sporadic at best, and would essentially remain so for the rest of his life.

Meanwhile, public demand for another moustached clown was on the rise.

---

* There are conflicting reports as to when Ciné Max Linder first opened. Walderkranz claims it to have been launched "as early as 1910," and the years 1917 and 1918 have also been suggested. However, late 1914 seems to be correct. See *La Presse*, December 16, 1914, or Renken, www.maxlinder.de/chronicleE.htm#1914. Also, a letter dated late 1914 with a header saying "Ciné Max Linder" is reproduced in one of Maud's books (Linder, Maud: *Les Dieux Du Cinéma Muet—Max Linder*, p. 91).

Èmile and Charles Pathé, as caricaturist A. Barriere saw them (1908). Author's collection.

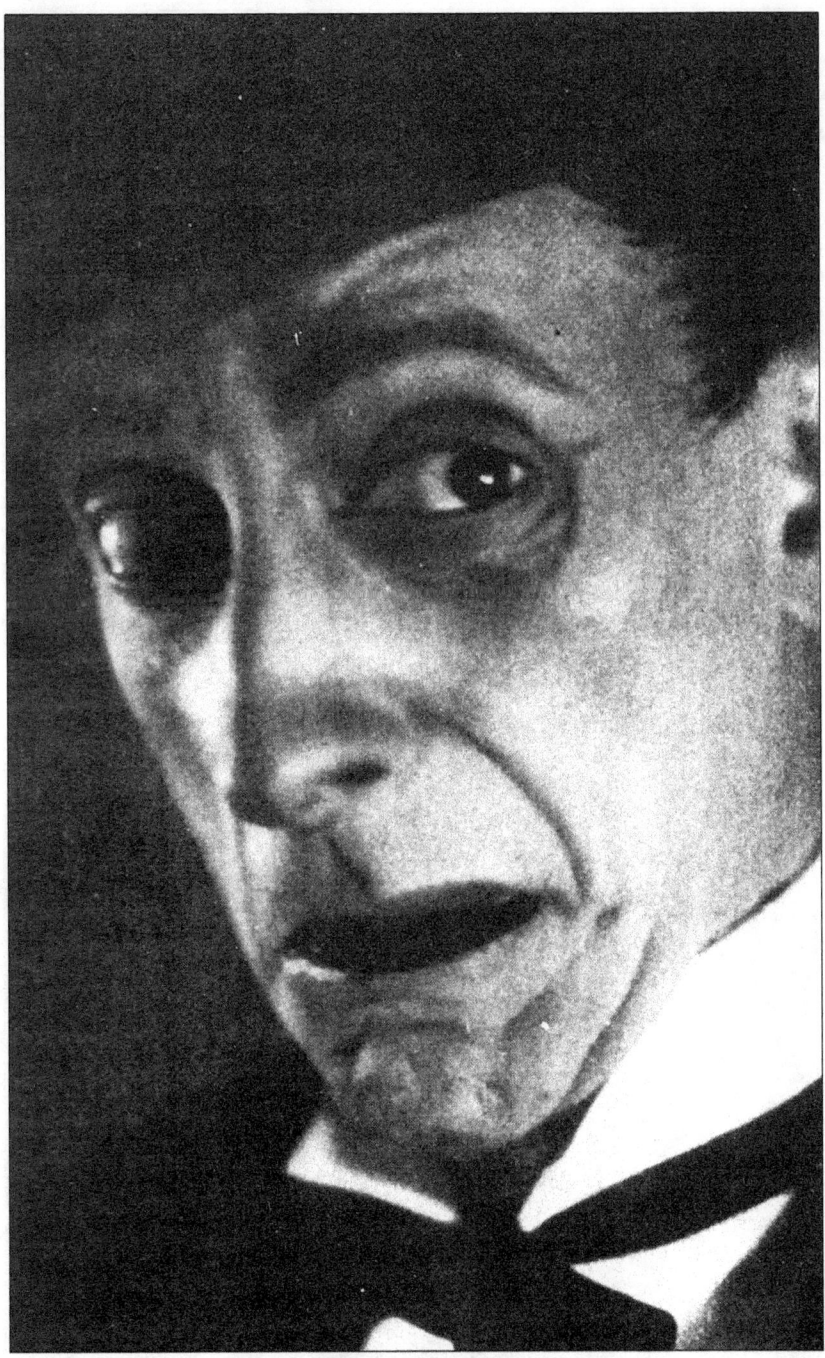

André Deed (1879-1940). Author's collection.

No hope in sight. Max in Les débuts d'un patineur *(1907). Author's collection.*

Soon *nauseous—*Le premier cigare d'un collégien *(His First Cigar, 1908). Author's collection.*

Charles Prince (1872-1933). Author's collection.

Superstar Max c. 1910. Author's collection.

Caught in a bathtub—Max prend un bain *(1910). Author's collection.*

On a bender. Max victime du quinquina *(1911), or* Max Takes Tonics. *Author's collection.*

Trendsetter Max—from Max lance la mode *(1912). Author's collection.*

Genuine friendship in Max et son chien Dick *(1912). Author's collection.*

Poster for Le duel de Max (1913), by all accounts the first full-length Max Linder film. Author's collection.

George K. Spoor (1871-1953). Author's collection.

Gilbert M. "Broncho Billy" Anderson (1880-1971). Author's collection.

He's back! From Max Comes Across *(1917). Author's collection.*

Martha Mansfield (1899-1923), leading lady in Max Linder's Essanay films. Author's collection.

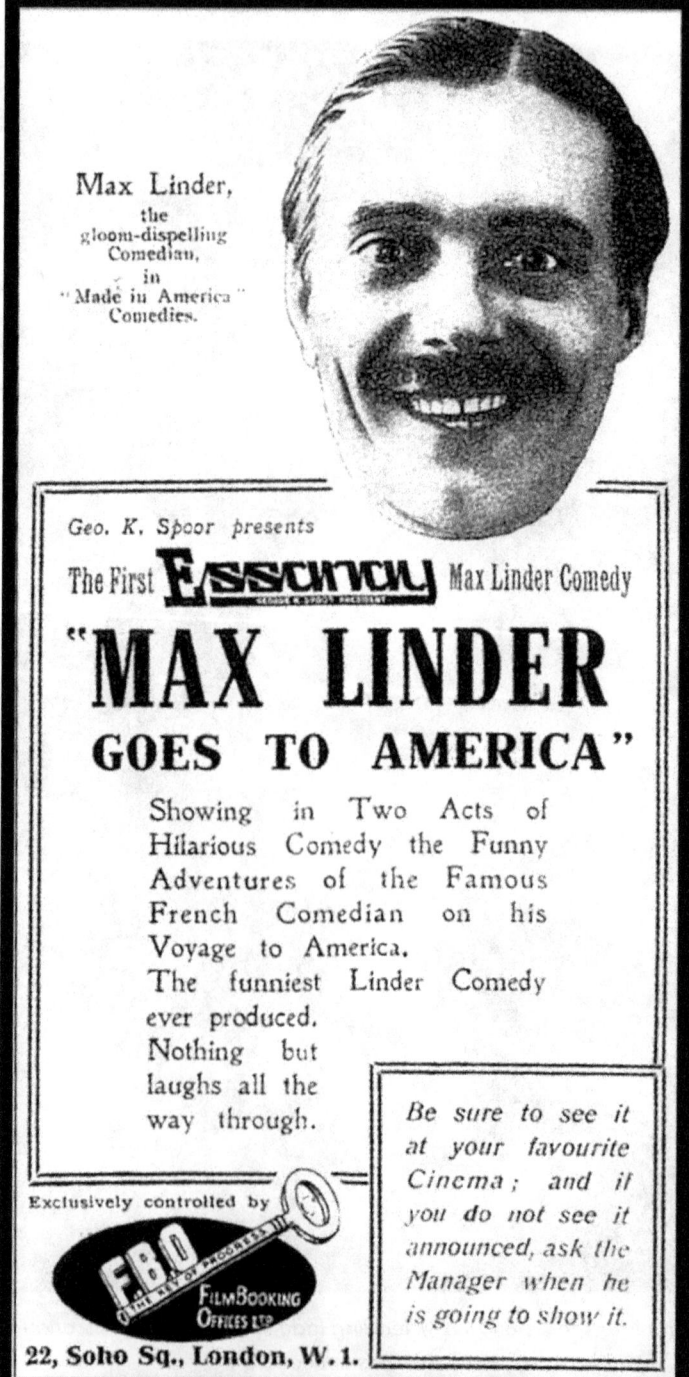

British ad for Max Comes Across (1917).

"Are You In For This Melon?" An ad for Max Linder's Essanay series, with a shot from Max in a Taxi (1917). Author's collection.

Max Linder visiting Charlie Chaplin's Lone Star Studio, May 1917. Author's collection.

On friendly terms—Max in the lion's cage in Seven Years Bad Luck (1921). Author's collection.

A most famous moment with Max Linder and Harry Mann doing the "mirror routine" in Seven Years Bad Luck (1921). Author's collection.

Unimpressed aunt—Alta Allen, Max Linder, and Caroline Rankin in Be My Wife *(1921). Author's collection.*

Oh, that Dart-In-Again! Max Linder (middle) in The Three Must-Get-Theres *(1922). Author's collection.*

Married—Linder and Ninette Peters, August 1923. Author's collection..

The sixth feature, a publicity still of Max, der Zirkuskönig *(1924). Author's collection.*

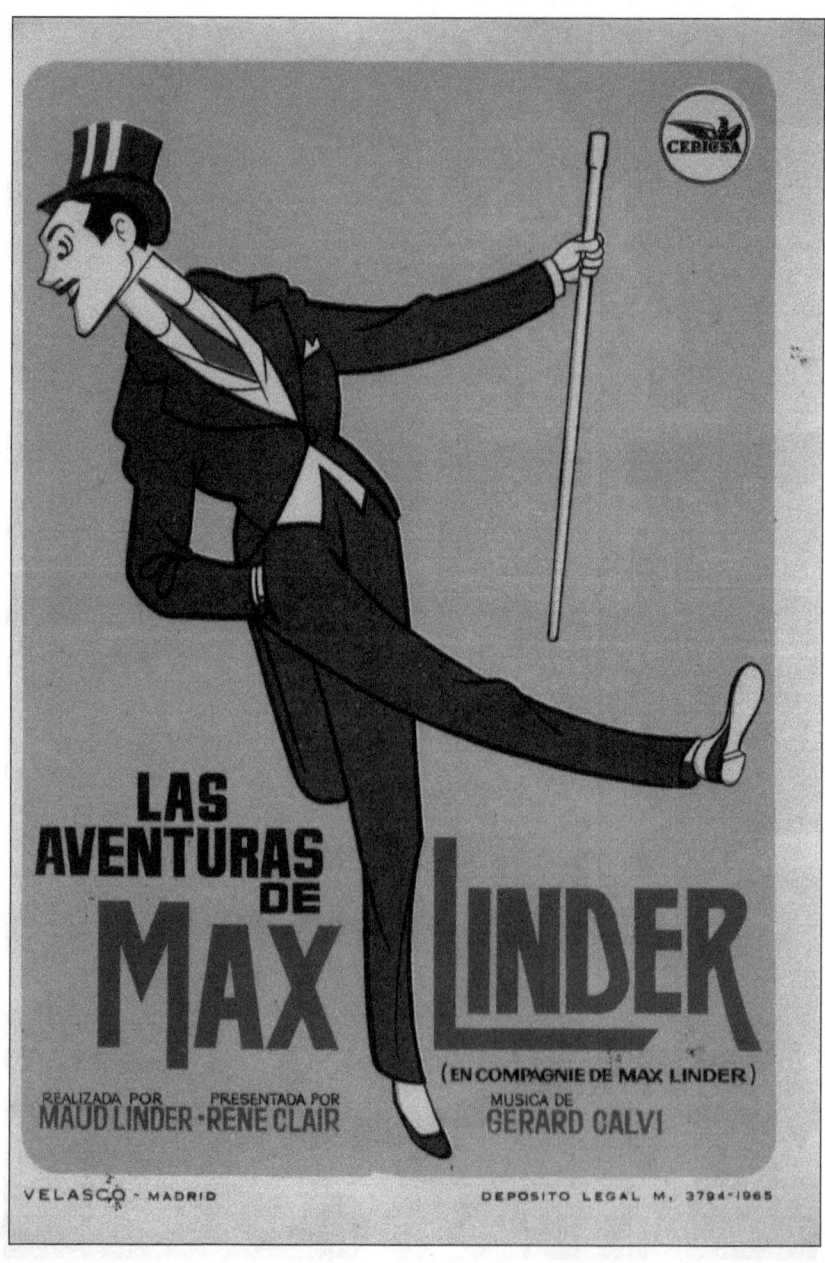

A Spanish poster for En compagnie de Max Linder *(1963). Author's collection.*

CHAPTER 14
MAX OPERATES IN THE STATES

Early 1915 saw the dawn of the Chaplin craze. The sudden popular boost of Chaplin's tramp character first swept Europe and the United States, soon spanning other continents with almost equal clout. In Max's home country, the tramp with the toothbrush moustache was to gather a particularly fervent following, as the French nearly from the onset bestowed on him the pet name of "Charlot."

Having survived an awful childhood rife with poverty and parental neglect, Charles Spencer Chaplin was six months into his second American tour with Fred Karno's pantomime ensemble, when he was asked by a New York Motion Picture Company representative to sign up with their Keystone Pictures Studios, thinking he could replace Fred Mace, a star who intended to leave. He signed a contract in September 1913. After his first film, *Making a Living* was released in February 1914, Chaplin found his classic outfit by his second film, *Mabel's Strange Predicament*, and went on to star in well over thirty one- and two-reelers (as well as the feature *Tillie's Punctured Romance*) within the year. When his contract came up for renewal, he asked for an increase to $1,000 a week, which Keystone's founder, Mack Sennett, refused. Chaplin thus left Keystone for the Essanay Studios, having secured for himself a contract of $1,250 a week instead. Within months, his popularity reached a level rivaled only by Mary Pickford.

If Max Linder was the first worldwide movie star, Chaplin was the first star to have had his image extended to other media on a massive scale. By late 1915, stores across the country brimmed with various (unauthorized) Chaplin merchandise, including statuettes, games, candy, and comic books. Although the most intensive phase of the Chaplin craze had faded by the early 1920s—as other comedians began to catch up with him, one might say—Chaplin would maintain the role of a "barometer" to whom others were compared for at least throughout the silent era. Whenever a new star comedian was on the rise in those years, he'd invariably be labeled as "the next Chaplin" or "Chaplin's new rival."

Certainly there was plenty of room for other comedians than Chaplin, to say the least, but Max Linder's former position as the #1 superstar slipped after he came back from military service. In fact, it was on rather shaky ground by now, especially since he would not appear in front of a camera for still a good while to come.

Tulips and Doppelgängers

A few more films that Max had done prior to his stint in the army had yet to be released by early 1915, however. The three-reel *Le sosie* (*Max's Double*) hit theaters on March 10, 1915. A lost film, this scenario seems to have featured him in a dual role of sorts, as he unexpectedly encounters a "doppelgänger." It's quite a pity that this film is missing, intriguing as it sounds in one reviewer's summary: "Even for those who are experienced in the trickery of the camera it will be ... difficult to say exactly how some of [these] scenes are done. Finally, mention should be made of a ... sensational duel [scene] in the dark which figures in the film. It is a really exciting incident which would almost justify one in describing [the film] 'Max's Double' as a dramatic farce. That it makes ... enthralling entertainment no one who sees the picture will deny."[130]

Next out (and last out, for now) was *Tulipe merveilleuse* (*Max's Marvelous Tulip*) on March 22. Although a print of this film appears to exist, it was not readily available to view as of 2017. One writer briefly but encouragingly summed it up as "[a] delightful little comedy scene ... so slight in texture that only such an artist as Max could have made anything of it at all."[131]

For the record, this farce seems to have had Max and his wife share a passion for botany. When Max comes across a particularly astounding flower, he tries to keep it a secret from his wife until it's hatched, somehow causing him to be wrongly accused of unfaithfulness.[132]

Touring yet again

For whatever reason, Max proved unable (or unwilling) to resume his work at Pathé upon his return home. This despite the fact that Pathé seems to have had few, if any more of his unreleased films ready for dispatch by this point. Instead, after two months of rest in Lausanne, Switzerland, the comedian embarked on another tour. On May 19, 1915, he appeared at the prestigious Dal Verme theater in Milano, Italy, where he reappeared the following four nights. After visiting Florence and Genoa, he arrived in Rome on May 27, headlining a comic sketch at the Teatro Nazionale. On the second day of this engagement, says Renken, "the Italian Prime Minister Antonio Salandra attend[ed] the performance."[133]

Upon Max's arrival in Italy, the country was still officially neutral in the war, much to France's dismay, but this had changed by the time he reached Rome, as war on Austria-Hungary was declared. As a result, his later stage appearances in the country were marked by a patriotic twist, as the comedian decided to hold brief speeches on the war. While in Florence, he declared that "I will return to [this city] when France has chased our common enemy," shouting "Long live Italy!... Long live France!" While Maud grants that his sentiments may now strike us as naïve, his words seem to have been appreciated at the time.[134]

Summer came and went, resulting in no new films for the comedian, and autumn fared little better. The two-reeler *Le hasard et l'amour* (*Max is Love Sick*) saw release on September 27, but Renken notes that this effort seems to have been shot two years prior.[135] It may have been somehow "forgotten" about on a shelf, or Max may have initially discarded it, but he now agreed to let Pathé release it as a compromise. Although he did arrive in Switzerland that month with the intention of shooting a film,[136] the ensuing effort, *Max victime de la main qui étreint* (*Max Wins and Loses*) wasn't ready for release until a year later.

While Chaplin was gaining new fans on a constant basis with films such as *The Tramp*, *The Bank*, and *A Night in the Show*, and Roscoe Arbuckle and Mabel Normand charmed audiences with such Keystone films as *Fatty and Mabel Adrift*, Max's admirers had to make do with reissues for the rest of 1915 and well into next year.

Another comeback

By early 1916, press reports revealed that Max had gone to Nice to "rest" for a while.[137] Nonetheless, on April 14 a new film finally hit the screens as *Deux août 1914* (August 2, 1914), its title referring to the last day of peace in France prior to its entrance in the war. Although the film was long thought to have been made in late summer 1914, Renken asserts this to be "highly unlikely,"[138] to which this author agrees. Instead, the completion of this one-reeler appears to have marked his comeback onscreen. Perhaps not surprisingly, the film dealt with the war, concluding with "a patriotic sentimental note," which, in the words of a French reviewer, "was not absolutely essential." Even so, the film was said to constitute "a rather amusing Max-Linder."[139] The comeback was also widely well-received in other countries, Norway included.

Max's health remained questionable, however. While Pathé was no doubt relieved to be handed *Deux août 1914*, the film proved a one-shot deal for the time being. The comedian instead spent the summer doing personal appearances for the allied troops. During this time, he seems to have suffered a "mental breakdown,"[140] presumably while in Lausanne, Switzerland, although the details are rather unclear. Maud states that, for the bulk of 1916, Max's life "remains for us in the shadows."[141]

A new enthusiasm for the screen accelerated by autumn, as George K. Spoor, president of the Essanay Studios in America, appeared on the scene[142] to make Max an offer he couldn't refuse. Having lost Chaplin to the Mutual Film Corporation a year before, Spoor appears to have been on the lookout for a replacement, and so he proposed to the comedian that he come to the United States to appear in a series of twelve two-reel comedies.[143] Max jumped on the opportunity, heading for Chicago in late October, though he made sure to get completed at least a few more films for Pathé prior to his takeoff, having presumably won back some of his earlier gusto.

Even in 1916, Essanay held a position as something of a veteran within the industry. Founded in 1907 by Spoor and Gilbert M. Anderson, the studio's legendary status was not confined to its association with Chaplin. Moreover, it had launched Anderson, its co-founder, as "Broncho Billy" Anderson, and as such, created the first Western star. Cross-eyed comedian Ben Turpin also worked at the studio for several years (although admittedly, he didn't become a star until later on). As it turned out, the company was soon to reach its salad days by the time Max came aboard, but was still ongoing as of yet.

The French comedian's arrival in the United States generated a fair chunk of publicity, both for Essanay and its new star. One paper reported: "France is contributing a substitute for Charley [sic] Chaplin in Max Linder, who will soon appear in Essanay pictures. Linder differs from Charley in [that he] disregard[s] [large] feet and cream pies as the essentials of [his] humor. Advance notices indicate that Linder believes pink or spotted pajamas to be the main prop of comedy."[144]

Of course this notice, likely written as tongue-in-cheek, greatly simplifies the essence of Chaplin and Max's comedy, to say the least (not that many pie-fights appeared in Chaplin's films, for one thing). However, the writer did arguably have a point in that Max's style differed somewhat from the more gag-driven humor of many (though not all) American comedians of 1916-1917. Despite Max's popularity in the United States, audiences likely expected some amount of adjustment on his part, a point that could not have passed him by, as his resulting efforts demonstrate.

As he settled down in Chicago a few weeks before Christmas, having brought his entire wardrobe with him from France, Max let the cameras roll on his first American production. Before its completion, Pathé saw fit to release some of the titles he had managed to get done in the past autumn. Following the release of *Max victime de la main qui étreint* in November, a production he had begun a year before, as noted above, the three-reeler *C'est pour les orphelins!* was brought to Ciné Max Linder in Paris on January 19, 1917. A charity film, this vehicle offered a total of nine sketches, each packed with various French stars, Max Linder and Charles Prince among them. Unfortunately, only a 3-minute version of the film is readily available today, which is sometimes erroneously assumed to be the whole thing.

Not counting the charity effort, the first two "conventional" Max Linder films of 1917, also leftovers from Pathé, both appear to have been released in Europe on February 16 as *Max et l'espion* (*Max and the Spies*) and *Max et le sac* (*Max Bags the Bloomer*), respectively. Warmly received in the press, one reviewer of the former film made sure to stress that it was "not a reissue."¹⁴⁵

A new phase—and new pace

The world was most of all awaiting Max's inaugural American comedy, and sure enough, on February 18, 1917 *Max Comes Across* premièred at the Strand Theatre, located near Times Square in New York City. Sadly, the film is unavailable (though not lost) today, but a synopsis suggests that Max's fondness for meta humor may have hit its apex with this effort. Almost as if anticipating the likes of Jack Benny and Jerry Seinfeld, Max is here said to have presented himself to us as, well, *himself*—what's more, in the opening scene, we presumably see him being persuaded to leave Paris for America (apparently by an Essanay deputy, no less).

The two-reeler mostly deals with his voyage onboard, providing a fair share of seasickness gags. Fearing shipwreck due to the ongoing war, Max has been hesitant about leaving home at first, and so, naturally, the farce escalates into a riot, as a war alarm goes off (which proves false in the end). The film's highlight is said to involve Max desperately playing on a sliding piano in the ship's saloon. In the end, he's declared a hero and gets the girl of his dreams, played by a teenage Martha Mansfield, here making her screen debut.*

Max Comes Across did spawn a predictable measure of attention, for sure. "NEW MAX LINDER FILM!" domestic and foreign ads boasted within the next couple of months.¹⁴⁶ Critics were not unanimous in their praise, however. While all had some good things to say about the film, there were several lukewarm reactions to be found. "Apparently Linder is as funny and as expressive [a comedian] as of yore," *Variety* said, "but the scenario for his first American-made release gives him small opportunity to exercise his well-known talents." This review's conclusion must have hit the comedian especially hard. "Future Essanay-Linder releases will have to be much funnier than [this] initial one if

---

* Billed Martha Early in Max Linder's Essanay films, Mansfield later became a minor star through such films as *Dr. Jekyll and Mr. Hyde* (1920) with John Barrymore. She tragically died of severe burns at the age of 24, after her dress caught fire from a match.

Linder is to rehabilitate himself as one of the world's foremost screen comedians," it was asserted.[147]

Another viewer found the comedian to be given "limited" opportunity to showcase "his indubitable . . . genius."[148] No doubt to Max's relief, at least one writer found his screen presence "irresistible," arguing that he seemed to have "grown in power as a magic mirth-maker since last seen."[149]

That Max had improved as a mirth-maker was also believed by the comedian himself for the time being, or at least that's the impression he gives in an interview conducted around the same time for the *Motion Picture Magazine*: "I think I am more capable now. I have had my sobs—now I will laugh with my audience."

The "sobs" referred to his war experiences, of course. The conversation also contained some rare reflections on how his months in the army had affected the comedian.

"Yes, monsieur; I am here again, sadder myself, but, I believe, more capable to make others laugh," he said. "It has been a terrible experience I have been thru. I have seen men suffer; I have seen men die; I have been close to death myself. You think, monsieur, that this experience would kill all the laughter in me? You are wrong. It has made me infinitely sad, but it has also taught me to laugh.

"There is one secret of laughter which I have learnt by this experience—the propinquity of laughter and tragedy.

"Soldiers, monsieur, learn to laugh. The horror of the battlefield is terrible. It is ghastly. To brood on it drives men mad.

"So, we learn to laugh, to take things as a matter of course. If we die, it is as it will be; if we live, we are glad. We laugh; we weep over the dead comrade; we rejoice over those who are living. So it is—the laughter and the tears are mingled together . . . .

"Ah, monsieur, when you hold the hand of a dying comrade, you know the grim tragedy of life. This great sadness has made me wish to bring more joy into the world. I want to make people laugh as never before.

"This experience has added a new element to my comedy; has taught me to inject a whimsical humor into tragedy—to bring laughter at the verge of tears...."

A sudden digression:

"You may smoke, monsieur; I enjoy the smell of a cigarette. But myself! I can smoke no more—the injury to my lung [during my service], monsieur. The doctor has told me never to touch the cigarette again. It is a hardship, but it is necessary.

"Also, I can eat very little. Pah! The physician found out all the things I liked to eat, and then cut them off the list. I eat mostly soups. I do not like them—these soups."

The conversation then moved to the subject of his upbringing:

"Yes, I have been on the stage. I started on the stage. But stage comedy and screen comedy are entirely different. One must think more to be successful on the screen. On the stage, one relies on the physical appearance, on the voice, on the wit and repartee of the play, as well as on personality. On the screen, you rely on your own action, on your own ability entirely, to express a thought or emotion. But it was hard for me to get on the stage. My parents were stage folk, but they did not want me to act. At twelve I was sent to a school in Bordeaux, where I was born, to be an artist. I did not like the work.

"[I was] indifferent with the brush, so I was sent to a musical conservatory. But I did not wish to study music. I wanted to be an actor.

"I was the naughty boy. I pretended to go to the music college, but instead attended a dramatic school. At the end of the year I won the first prize.*

Having summed up his years at Pathé, he then went on to reminisce more about his army stint and to describe the dramatic incident where he caught pneumonia after having, presumably, hidden in icy water from a German patrol. He concluded:

"I was sent back to the Contrexville hospital, and it was there I was asked to come to America.

"It was the inspiration. I had seen all the sorrows of the world. 'I will now try to bring more joy into it,' I said. "So I agreed to come to America. Here I am, monsieur. I have never been in America before. But I am back working for the screen, working to make people laugh, monsieur. I hope to succeed...."[150]

Although Max here gives the impression that Essanay had first contacted him while he was resting at the military hospital of Contrexville, France, this is contradicted by the timeline. After all, he had been discharged from the army about eighteen months prior to Essanay's offer. In my opinion, it seems rather to have been the case that Essanay had presented him with a contract while he was recovering from the "nervous breakdown" of the year before, as noted earlier, and, most likely, he simply wished to avoid going into the breakdown during this interview, thus putting the blame for his hospitalization entirely on war injuries.

---

* If true, this particular anecdote seems significant to our understanding of Max's years at the Conservatoire Muncipal de Bordeaux. However, as of now, I have not been able to verify his claim that he pretended to study music during his time there.

Incidentally, the conversation appears have taken place with an "interpreter" on hand, as Max's English was said to be rather "broken."

By the time *Max Comes Across* hit the screens, the comedian's second American film was already nearing completion. On March 18, *Max Wants a Divorce* saw release, once more at New York's Strand Theatre. Again teamed up with young Martha Early-Mansfield, Max here finds himself happily married. However, the family peace is soon interrupted as he receives a telegram from his rich uncle demanding that our hero stay a bachelor or otherwise he'll disinherit him (yes, *that* premise again). Max is met with quite a scolding (involving flying furniture) as he suggests to his wife that they divorce. However, he soon wins her over as he promises that they'll remarry later, and he'll buy her a precious string of pearls for her trouble.

In those days, of course, you'd better have a good reason to demand divorce, and so Max sets out to commit "adultery" with his wife's blessing. They rent an empty apartment, whereupon Max seduces an unsuspecting female at a party. Meanwhile, the wife calls a private detective, telling him that her husband may soon be found making love to another woman in said apartment. Around the same time, a Freudian-like psychiatrist is setting up office in the apartment next door. When the detective arrives to investigate the "adultery" case, he's naturally mistaken for a mental patient, and quite a mayhem ensues.

The film's mockery of the "mental patients" towards the end feels like over-the-top buffoonery, and is frankly quite heartless: one man believes himself to be an automobile, and that kind of stuff. Nonetheless, *Max Wants a Divorce* does have its moments, for sure, with a typically engaging performance by Max.

Variety, for one, was more positive this time around, stating that "[t]he comedy should be a welcome addition to any program as the slapstick work is not overdone and fits with the development of the piece."[151]

Others were sympathetic, as well. One observed that "[t]he speedy French comedian never worked faster nor more amusingly than in *Max Wants a Divorce*."[152] Upon its reissue two years later, a Norwegian reviewer labeled the two-reeler a "harmless [but] quite amusing" farce; "Max Linder naturally puts heaven and earth in motion," the writer declared, "as is his wont."[153]

Five weeks later, on April 23, *Max in a Taxi* premièred. Whereas Max's previous two films were shot in Chicago, this one was made in sunny California. In one press report, it was said that the "reason for Max's departure was pressure for floor space at the [Essanay] Chicago studio," and thus "[p]lans were launched a month [before] for the selection of another studio exclusively for Linder's use."[154]

The resulting effort, *Max in a Taxi*, stands as the Essanay comedy with the least plot. When Max arrives home on a bender, his wealthy father decides he's had enough and throws the son out, possibly for good. With no money on him to speak of, our hero then thinks it best to kill himself (!). Spotting a coming train in the distance, he lies down on the railroad track, preparing for eternal rest. Of course, the engine shifts course at the last moment. Next he tries to hang himself, with no more luck.

As he stumbles upon an invitation to a dance party, however, he suddenly finds life worth living after all. Once at the party, he overindulges in a bowl of creampuffs, before making the acquaintance of a charming lady (Martha Early-Mansfield again). Later on, our hero is appointed the job of taxi driver (thus the film's title), which leads him to again bump into Martha and her mother, offering them a ride that soon turns disastrous as the car runs amok. Finally crashing, Max literally flies up in the air, and in the last shot, we see him balancing on a batch of telephone wires above, grinning and still wearing his top hat.

One reviewer found *Max in a Taxi* "inferior to the two previous Linder comedies."[155] However, by and large, critics were pleased. A favorable comparison was made between *Max in a Taxi* and Chaplin's *One A.M.* (1916).[156]

Moving Picture World went out of its way to declare Max an artist: "Everybody knows that [he is an artist] . . . [this] reviewer has been writing about Max off and on for the last six years. Max's art is always fresh . . . The wonder is that he still has new things [left] in his box of wonders, but he has."[157]

Although the box office receipts for Max's Essanays are not known to this author, the films seem not to have rivaled the product of other comedy stars to a great degree, Essanay's shrewd publicity machine notwithstanding. It is perhaps telling that a program ad of the time found room to mention one of Max's new films only in an apropos—announcing in a lower right corner, "Also Max Linder in 'Max Wants a Divorce,'" while a reissue of an old Chaplin film was treated with bold letters in the same ad, accompanied by a full-size still of Chaplin in costume.*

Sadly, as Max struggled to regain his work ethic amidst various health issues, he found that he no more drew the box office magic of five years prior. That said, it's important to put things in perspective: Max was still star material, for sure, more in demand than a great many others of his profession, yet the public's craving for Chaplin, Arbuckle, and soon Harold Lloyd, was of a vaster nature by now.

A fourth Essanay film was scheduled for production—Max having apparently outlined its scenario—but it was not to be. As early as March, shortly before completion of *Max in a Taxi*, *Variety* had gossiped that "all is not happy in the Essanay camp regarding Max Linder, and the story has it that George K. Spoor has attempted several times lately to unload his high-priced contract with the fastidious French star ... Neither of the first two [Essanay-Linder] releases has [sic] developed anything like the interest that was expected. An error in the way Linder['s] publicity was mapped out has [had] something to do with the lukewarm reception of [his] new comedies. ... Spoor is supposed to have originally obtained Linder in an attempt to spite Charlie Chaplin [!]. When Chaplin left Essanay[,] the [studio] still had Charlie's [film] "Carmen" [left to be released], which was [originally] made [by Chaplin] for two reels [but was] then padded out by Essanay to make a four-reeler. Thereupon Chaplin sued Spoor, with the result that the Essanay head became angry and went scouting for an 'opposition' comic. This resulted in bringing Linder to this country."[158]

---

* See *The Lake County Times*, April 13, 1917. The Chaplin reissue, incidentally, was *The Knockout* (1914), actually a Roscoe Arbuckle vehicle with Chaplin doing a cameo appearance.

The claim that Spoor had initially sought out Max in a conscious attempt to "spite Charlie Chaplin" should probably be taken with a grain of salt, though it is certainly true that Chaplin and Essanay had not parted on friendly terms. Readers familiar with Chaplin's career will know the story, of course: as his last effort for Essanay in late 1915, Chaplin had set out to make a burlesque on Cecil B. DeMille's film, *Carmen* (1915). As the note above explains, the comedian had originally cut it as a two-reeler, but after he departed from the company in early 1916 before the film's release, Essanay wound up practically bastardizing the effort, expanding it into four reels by inserting outtakes and newly shot footage. Chaplin was so enraged by this that he had to spend two days in bed, and he went to court (to no avail).[159] However, while it seems plausible that Spoor had indeed perceived Max as a replacement to Chaplin, as has often been claimed, this was likely most initiated by a wish to make money on his part, rather than thirst for "revenge" on Charlie.

Yet, Essanay had clearly expected more profit from the French star than they got. According to one later press item, Spoor "wrote off a loss of $87,000 on the Linder adventure."[160] Nonetheless, it would seem exceptionally naïve for the company to have imagined that Max, who had not made films on a regular basis since 1914, should have been able to instantly compete with Chaplin's popularity. Indeed, while Spoor is believed to have terminated Max's contract due to disappointing box office receipts, the comedian's health issues likely played a role, as well. At least that's the impression given in a report in the spring, stating that Max "is unable to proceed with his motion picture work for Essanay." He was said to be "suffering from stomach trouble, resulting from shrapnel wounds he received in France."[161] Later reports of the year were also to maintain that Linder was indeed seriously ill.

Viewed today, at least one of Max's two Essanay films available for viewing holds up quite well, in this author's opinion (as noted above, I've been unable to track down the first effort, *Max Comes Across*, unfortunately). More fast-paced both in action and editing than had been his custom at Pathé, it's clear that the comedian had studied the jesters of America with interest, many of whom had no doubt been influenced by himself at one point. On the other hand, perhaps he had let himself be a bit elated by the antics of the American stars. For fun, though these two-reelers remain, exceptional they are not. Max is not three years ahead of everyone else here, as he had very arguably been around 1911. Again, in the author's opinion, *Max Wants a Divorce* is probably the better effort—it's certainly the more polished in terms of story construction, presenting Max as his usual likable self, and allowing for some nice visual touches, such as a sequence with he and his wife arguing in silhouette. *Max in a Taxi* looks quite rushed by comparison. His rambling actions in the film are completely unmotivated, for one thing, but even if one accepts that, much of its comic business feels like standard fare. Max's deteriorating health had likely contributed to its quick wrap-up.

Professor—and Disciple

At least one more fruitful encounter was to come out of Max's stay in America. In May, the comedian dropped by Charlie Chaplin's Lone Star Studio in Hollywood, where the latter was then finishing his two-reel comedy, *The Adventurer* (1917). The two stars got along swell, by all accounts. During this visit, Chaplin famously presented Max with a portrait of himself, inscribed: *"To the one and only Max, 'The Professor,' From his Disciple—Charlie Chaplin."* On his part, Max freely expressed his admiration for Chaplin on a later occasion, declaring the younger comedian's efforts to be "so impressive that one cannot exaggerate [his] impact. He calls me his teacher, but I have been the happy one to take lessons from his 'school'. . . . Any moviegoer regardless of origin . . . will immediately grasp Chaplin's message and the refined nuances of his humor."[162]

Chaplin's inscription to Max has become the stuff of legend to silent comedy fans, and is often taken as definite proof of Max's impact on the younger star. Of course, one may argue that Chaplin had likely been in a good mood on the occasion, and saw it fit to acknowledge that Max had been in the game longer than himself, regardless of any influence. That said, there can be little doubt that Chaplin had seen at least some of Max's farces while still a youngster, and that the Frenchman's work—directly or indirectly—had taught him a thing or two about comedy construction on film. There are also similarities to be found between the two comedians as performers, for sure; they're both exceptional mimes, blessed with large, expressive eyes and impeccable timing. Whether their resemblances are coincidental, or if Chaplin indeed was directly influenced by Max early on, is probably a matter of debate. Chaplin does not mention Max in his much later memoirs, but French Linder-biographer Charles Ford cites a quote attributed to Chaplin, wherein he admits to have "created [the Tramp] by borrowing from the great French comic a few details of attitude and dress."[163]

Ultimately, the respective *characters* of the two do set them quite apart. Whereas Chaplin's tramp developed into a symbol of the "little man"—the outsider always striving for acceptance, if only for a moment at a time—Max's *boulevardier* was invariably well set up in life, seldom suffering any major issues to speak of. The tramp triggers our curiosity. *Where does this mysterious little creature come from, anyway? Who are his parents?* Max, however, may not carry such a secretive aura about him. No less is it striking how he manages to make us care about his seemingly more conventional character. Like the tramp, Max is truly funny in and of himself, but he's also peculiarly *human*, with an often poetic streak to his presence. Even in his less remarkable works of the early 1910s, he comes off as more charismatic, I dare say, than any other film comedian working at that particular time. Very early on, he recognized the impact of audience interaction in his performances with his frequent grins and winks to the public, often coupled with a spontaneous little dance in the midst of a scene, which, to a large degree, explain his lasting appeal.

With no more American offers in sight, at least for now, Max left the United States by late summer, boarding the ship *Espana* on August 11, 1917. Sadly, his health had seen better days.

CHAPTER 15
MAX'S REIGN WANES

As reports of his declining health had piled up throughout spring and summer 1917, one wonders how audiences responded to the release of no less than three new Max-pictures within the remainder of that year: *Max entre deux feux* (*Max, the Heartbreaker*) in May, Max, médecin malgré lui in September, and Max devrait porter des bretelles in November.* Since the public at large was likely unaware that these cheerful two-reelers had, in fact, been shot the preceding autumn as his final assignments at Pathé prior to his departure for America, fans of the comedian may not have felt fully forlorn by words of his health struggles. If so, this presumably changed by the end of October, with one Norwegian paper bleakly proclaiming:

"Max Linder Is Dying

"There is hardly a person alive who does not know the name of Max Linder. Some years ago, he occupied the same position . . . which Charles Chaplin by now has conquered. . . . Many an alarming rumor has circulated throughout the war years stating that Max Linder is dead, fallen on the battlefield. . . . But the popular actor has survived the war. He was indeed called up to the front, proving himself a brave and daring soldier."

The article then briefly outlines his recent stint in the United States, concluding:

"But not many [more] films were to be made. Linder had overestimated his health. . . . [H]e had to give up filming, and traveled to California in the hope that the sunny

---

* I have not found any official English titles for the latter two films.

climate would do him good. However, doctors now attest that Max has few more months to live, and so he has left America to die in his beloved France.

"A somber end to a life whose purpose has been to cheer others."[164]

The exact same notice was repeated in a smaller Norwegian paper three days later,[165] which could imply that the piece had been copied from a foreign source. Once again, prophecies of Max's demise proved false, and were quickly forgotten in Norwegian and international press alike, but the comedian was indeed to remain idle for a good while to come. While reissues of his old films still appeared on movie screens all over Europe, coverage of his personal life now came to a halt for a time.

Early spring 1918 brought good news, however, as *Motion Picture News* announced that the comedian would return to the United States "in April or May":

"[Linder] intends to make a new series of pictures, for which he will engage the support of a capable company. In all probability, the stories will be prepared by Tom Bret, [a] scenario and title writer.... Satisfied that he has now so fully recovered his health and strength as to permit him to resume active studio work, M. Linder ... has signified his intention of returning here in a month or two. It is not yet decided whether he will appear under the auspices of a producing organization or make his own productions for distribution through a large releasing syndicate."[166]

As promising as it sounds, with the experienced comedy writer and editor, Tom Bret, on board as assistant, this message also soon turned out to be misleading. An American comeback for Max would eventually materialize, but not at this time. In fact, he was not to appear in a new film for two whole years, by far his longest screen absence to date. During the same stretch, Chaplin produced two of his best-loved films, the three-reelers *A Dog's Life* and *Shoulder Arms* (both 1918), while bespectacled Harold Lloyd was gaining widespread notice in a highly successful series of one-reelers. Roscoe Arbuckle kept an equally busy schedule, churning out his own series of bi-monthly two-reelers, each title being more erratic than the previous one. Although still a name of renown, Max Linder must have recognized that he was unlikely to sustain his worldwide fame if he remained in Europe for long. World War I had hit the European film industry hard, and though it was to survive, producing an infinite number of exceptional talents in the decades to come, superstars now belonged in the United States. Granted, Max's one-time rival, Charles Prince, still starred in reasonably popular short comedies in France, but he could no longer compete with the giants of Hollywood by a long shot.

It must have been of some further disappointment to Max that his final three films to be released before his two-year break—the aforementioned *Max entre deux feux* (*Max the Heartbreaker*), *Max, médecin malgré*, and *Max devrait porter des bretelles*—all received somewhat indifferent reviews. Thankfully, thoroughly negative the critics were not.

Of these three films, *Max entre deux feux* (*Max the Heartbreaker* is the most easily accessible for viewing today. One reviewer found "the comedy element [in this film] ... rather slow in coming, but when it comes Max gets over a full share of laughs."[167]

The film presents Max not at his most likable, perhaps. As two girls both find themselves crazy about our hero, they decide to fight "a duel to the death." Max is delighted by the attention, and eagerly climbs up a tree to watch the outcome. In the end, of course, it's our top-hatted friend who receives a bullet (though not with fatal results). The film's funniest moment occurs about halfway through its two reels, and is not of real relevance to the main plot: as Max strolls about in the park, he finds himself a spot on a bench in between a stately couple, but soon discovers that he's not welcome and moves on. On the way, he stumbles over an apple on the ground. Tempted by the sight of the fruit, he takes a juicy bite and throws it backwards, so that it hits the gentleman on the bench behind him. The furious man throws it back in Max's direction, of course, but our friend gallantly catches it, takes another bite, and throws it back yet again. This time, it hits the lady's scalp. She believes her husband responsible and a violent brawl follows. Meanwhile, Max swaggers down the road with glee.

Reviewing his next film, *Max, médecin malgré*, a French critic came off as less enthusiastic: the film "is not one of Max Linder's best comedies," he wrote, "and surprisingly, as . . . Linder's scenarios are generally [well] studied, this comic scene is full of mistakes in its staging. To describe them . . . it would be necessary to analyze a whole scenario that has to have been written hastily and turned out even faster, while . . . Linder made his trunks ready to go to the country of dollars [America] . . ."[168]

This last point confirms that at least a few critics were aware that Max's last films of 1917 had been shot shortly before his American departure.

Max devrait porter des bretelles gained more positive reactions, in so far as the film was reviewed at all. Again, a French reviewer began his review by briefly lamenting Max's now limited productivity, declaring the film an "all too rare Max." Though the writer wasn't quite sure if the two-reeler was indeed a new film or a reissue (by all accounts, it was, in fact, a brand new product), he found it to be a "[g]ood picture." Incidentally, this film seems to have included a scene involving a "false Charlot."[169] – Unfortunately, I have not been able to investigate this point further, though copies of it are known to still exist.

Charity gala—and more "rest"

An uncertain future notwithstanding, Max did manage to get some work done within 1918. Renken cites a "[c]harity gala for soldiers . . . suffering from tubercolosis," held "at the Grand-Théâtre in Lausanne" Switzerland in late May. Max appears to have performed two sketches onstage, entitled *Le baromètre de la fidélité* and *L'addition*, respectively. Five weeks later, he was featured in "yet another charity event" in Lausanne, this time advertised as 'Gala Max Linder.'[170]

That, however, was it for the year's remainder. As far as anyone knows, Max was not involved in any more professional activities until well into 1919. It's hard not to speculate if he hadn't suffered another breakdown of sorts. The comedian had been in Lausanne a few years before, as noted earlier, and Maud assumes his collapse of 1916 to have occurred while there.[171] Since no medical records of him from this period have surfaced as of this writing, it remains unclear if he, in fact, suffered *two* separate breakdowns, both during or around the time of his visits to Lausanne in 1916 and 1918, or if there has been a mixup of events in later accounts. His alleged "mental breakdowns"— a diffuse diagnosis that by now has been abandoned as a medical term— have been clouded by no small amount of mystery through the years. One is left to ponder whether his condition was caused mostly by physical or mental pains, or both. In any case, it can be safely assumed that his lack of output during 1918-1919 had sound reasons. His American journey of the year before verifies that his creative vein was still intact.

Thankfully, at least a temporary upswing was to occur by next year's end.

CHAPTER 16
MAX'S KEEN RETURN TO THE SCREEN

On June 28, 1919, the Treaty of Versailles was signed, officially ending World War I. The dismal prediction of British Army officer Herbert Kitchener had proven true that the global battle had indeed lasted for four years.[172] An estimated 17 million people lost their lives, and still more were wounded.

For Max, the war's closure partly meant the end of a limited international distribution of his films, although this was of little consequence to him at first, given his screen hiatus.

Feature play, yet again

Pathé had not given up on their past superstar, however. They bought the screen rights to famed author Tristan Bernard's play, *Le petit café*, and by autumn, Max set out to star in his first film in two years. What's more, the new production was also to be his second feature-length effort, running at roughly 75 minutes.* The comedian was not to play a major role behind the scenes, for a change. Instead, Bernard's son, Raymond, stepped in as director.** With filming wrapping up in October, Max intently awaited its reception.

Although Bernard's successful three-act play had been first staged in Paris in 1911, its most famous rendition had perhaps occurred in America, where it was presented as a musical comedy a few years later. The knowledge that its songs would be lost to silent film may have contributed to a relative disinterest in Max's new film as far as United States audiences were concerned. However, by all accounts, *Le petit café* (*The Little Café*) did fine business in Europe upon and beyond its release in Paris on December 19, 1919. The scenario presents Max as a waiter at The Little Café, but no common waiter at that. He is, in fact, heir to an uncle's considerable fortune. Problems arise when one of the

---

* When played at 24 fps.
** As noted in Chapter 2, Raymond Bernard (1891-1977) was to eventually direct Max's onetime friend, Max Dearly, in *Les misérables* (1934).

uncle's old servants learns of the inheritance, as the servant slyly seeks out Max's boss at the Café, and convinces him to sign Max up for twenty years as a waiter. What's more, he makes the boss add a precondition saying that anyone who breaks the arrangement shall spit up 500,000F on the table. Even as Max eventually learns of his coming inheritance, then, he's forced to remain at The Little Café, or else have to pay the fortune.

Long-running films had become a well-established phenomenon since Max's first feature of six years prior. In 1919 alone, audiences were treated to such multi-reel vehicles as *Daddy-Long Legs* with Mary Pickford, *When the Clouds Roll By* with Douglas Fairbanks, and D. W. Griffith's *Broken Blossoms* with Richard Barthelmess and Lillian Gish, to name a few. American filmmakers knew how to make longer movies by this time, which was hinted at, somewhat disparagingly, in a review of Max's new film: "[h]ad the picture been produced by an American director," it was said, "more attention would have been paid to the romantic element [in the film], which is very poorly developed here."[173] For the record, Max was, in fact, paired with a leading lady in *Le petit café*, a 27-year old actress named Wanda Lyon.*

Nonetheless, most audiences enjoyed the movie. One American exhibitor remarked that "[i]ts comedy sequences are good when they appear." Furthermore, playhouses running the feature were encouraged to "make a point of announcing that it marks the return to the screen of Max Linder, most popular comedian in France, after a long absence due to illness from war injuries." In addition, though his new film may have played better in Europe, there was no doubt that the comedian had "many admirers in this country [as well,] and this first reappearance should attract [many] from old time's sake." The note also made clear that the film "was made in Paris and . . . contains many scenes shot on that city's streets."[174]

European critics were still more excited. In the opinion of an Austrian reviewer, the feature gave "the brilliant comedian opportunity to play out all of his abilities," and to "put all nuances of

---

* Primarily a stage actress, with *Le petit café*, Wanda Lyon (1892-1976) made her first out of only three known screen appearances.

his art into the service of his role." He found much of the comedy "extremely funny," while it also offered "numerous fine-grained situations in which the faces [of the audience] can be smoothed to a quiet smile, [as they are] recovering from the exertions of laughter." Lastly, the Austrian writer seemed to find no fault with the film's romantic element, judging the "scenes with his affectionate partner Miss Wanda Lyon" to be filled with "a fine sense of humor and real poetry."[175]

Pleased though he no doubt was by its mostly enthusiastic response, Max had not been present at the French premiére of *Le petit café*. By mid-November, he had already left the country for another transatlantic journey.

Once again, the Land of Opportunity awaited him.

CHAPTER 17
MAX SCORED WITH A SWORD

Half a year seems to have passed before the cameras again rolled – but by spring 1920, shooting began on Max's first American feature-length film, produced as part of the newly-founded Max Linder Productions. Robertson-Cole served as the film's distributor.

This time, Max had set up shop in Los Angeles, once again occupying the director's chair. However, as its budget was derived from French funds, the upcoming film would be considered a foreign production in America,[176] which unfortunately meant a more limited distribution in the country. As he still suffered from dire health, adapting to the pace of Hollywood proved challenging. In several letters written home to his mother during these months, he bluntly despaired over his situation, confessing to be spending "truly awful days."[177]

There was a language barrier to be considered, as well. His mastery of the English language still limited, he made his ideas "known through a combination of French and gestures" while directing.[178] Among his assistants on the production was Charles Dorian, who was soon to become a trusted Second Unit Director in Hollywood. Charles Van Enger was hired as cameraman.

Back again—with *Seven Years Bad Luck*

Despite all the difficulties, Max managed to get his new feature, *Seven Years Bad Luck*, done by August. Upon its release in Los Angeles on February 6, 1921, the 65-minute comedy had already received some decent notices. Having attended a preview screening held the preceding autumn, one exhibitor called it "a fun film that will please any audience," with "[o]ne of its charms [being] that it seems more like a two-reeler than a five[-reeler], because of the snappiness of the action."[179]

Whether the "short film feeling" of the feature is a strength, as believed by the exhibitor above, or a potential weakness, may be a matter of debate. There is at least no doubt that the film follows a rather vague storyline: having broken a large mirror during his morning shave, Max believes himself haunted by seven years of bad luck. As his fiancée rejects him later on the same day (due to some childish behavior on his part), our hero decides to embark on a long journey to get away from it all. A good portion of the film takes place on a train, as Max heads for some unknown destination. Several mishaps later, he finds himself seeking refuge from a group of furious cops in a lion's cage. The animals turn out to rather like our hero, and so he's safe for a while, though eventually the clumsy officers get their hands on him, and he's thrown in prison. While waiting for his trial before the judge (at least that's how this author interprets the scene—it's not entirely clear what's going on at this point), our hero spots his ex-fiancée in the court, about to get hitched with a rival suitor of his. Understandably enraged, he somehow gets himself out of the mess and wins back the girl. In the final scene, seven years later, the couple is seen happily exiting their stately home with a total of seven urchins following their path, all dressed up as "mini-Maxes" (top hats included).

One thing is certain: it's admirable how the real-life Max manages to suppress his health-related worries while onscreen, with seeming ease at that. He is thoroughly engaging to watch throughout, his oft-repeated grin as irresistible as ever. There is also some inspired comic business going on here, for sure; as noted above, in the first reel he famously revisited the "mirror routine," the act that had brought his first feature, *Le duel de Max*, legal trouble back in 1913. Thankfully, this time the routine was allowed to stay intact wherever the film was screened. It may be redundant to describe it at length, but here goes: Max's valet and maid are enjoying some flirtatious play one morning while their master still slumbers, when all of a sudden a full-size mirror is smashed. Dreading their master's reaction, the two convince the chef of the house to dress up in one of Max's pajamas, and place himself behind the broken mirror's frame so that when the master enters to do his morning shave, he'll take the chef for his own mirror image. The resemblance between the two men is sufficient enough to pull it off, and within the next seven to eight minutes, a snippet of golden silent comedy is brought before us. While the routine had become more widely-known by 1921 than what had been the case eight years prior—with Chaplin and Harold Lloyd having staged their own takes on it by now* —Max no doubt spent a fair amount of time bringing it to such meticulous perfection as seen here. His interplay with the "chef" (played by Russian-born actor Harry Mann) is beyond reproach, and remains both genuinely impressive and a real joy to watch.

Owing in part to the relatively frequent showings of *Seven Years Bad Luck* at film festivals in the past few decades (as opposed to other films by Max), the "mirror routine" stands as the comedian's most famous moment to this day. Without question, the routine also constitutes the highlight of this particular feature. Entertaining though it remains to the end, *Seven Years Bad Luck* seems to be a film largely made in the editing room, perhaps more reliant on afterthoughts than careful planning as far as its story is concerned.

Film comedies spanning more than an hour in length were still looked upon as hazy terrain when Max commenced this production in the spring of 1920. While a moderate number of comedians (and comediennes) had made the "transition" from shorts to features already—among them Mabel Normand with *Mickey* (1918), and even Max's one-time rival, Charles Prince in France—it was still the consensus that "slapstick" comedy could not normally sustain an audience's interest for several reels at a time. As a consequence, most comedy features made up to around 1920 were of the "light" variety, that is, more dramatic vehicles with comic touches than outright laugh riots. This attitude also pertained when Roscoe "Fatty" Arbuckle, second only to Chaplin in popularity among slapstick jesters in the late 1910s, made his first full-length films at Paramount, with titles such as *The Round-Up* and *The Life of the Party* (both 1920). In the opinion of many critics and historians, two films of the early 1920s almost single-handedly proved to the industry at large that spectators were more than willing to sit through a multi-reel "slapstick" film, if done well: Chaplin's *The Kid* (1921) and Harold Lloyd's *Grandma's Boy* (1922).

---

* Chaplin in *The Floorwalker* (1916); Lloyd in *The Marathon* (1919).

These two films, for all their memorable comedy sequences, were perhaps most notable for their deft integration of suspense and character development along with their comic moments. As smash hits of the day, both had, by all accounts, significant impact on the comedy industry for years to come.

Given that Chaplin's The Kid, by a curious coincidence, was released a mere week before Seven Years Bad Luck, Max's feature must be considered a pioneering work, a film made still before the real breakthrough of feature-length comedies, and judging by that criteria, it holds up rather well. Other than the mirror scene, a sequence at a train station, where Max shrewdly avoids paying for his ticket by shadowing a larger man, and the business in the lion's cage, are quite delightful. On the other hand, Max's relationship with his fiancée in the film, played by actress Alta Allen, feels underdeveloped. She is given little opportunity to do anything but simply look sweet in her role.*

Reactions to Seven Years Bad Luck were largely positive. One reviewer called it a "clean and enjoyable comedy," with a "catchy" title that "should attract picture-patrons."[180] By all accounts, the feature did only fair business at the box office, probably in part due to its (certainly questionable) status as a "foreign" production.

Be My Wife

Following the première of Seven Years Bad Luck in the winter, Max quickly went ahead on another American feature, and by June 1921, Be My Wife was ripe for release, save for a few additional edits. Even more episodic in structure than his previous effort, the highlight of this film must also be said to occur within its first fifteen minutes or so. Happily in love with a girl named Mary (once again played by Alta Allen), Max struggles for the approval of the girl's domineering aunt (Caroline Rankin**). Having disguised himself as his sweetheart's long-bearded music teacher

---

* Alta Allen (1904-1979) seems to have made her screen debut with Seven Years Bad Luck. She was to reappear with the comedian in his next feature, and went on to perform in a few more films up to 1926.

** A memorable screen presence, Rankin (1880-1953) was typically cast in bossy female roles throughout the 1920s, making her last screen appearance in 1939.

(a premise he'd visited years before in the short film *La maîtresse de piano* (1908), although then in drag), our hero is eventually busted by the lively family dog and has to make a swift escape. Not one to give up, later in the evening, he decides on a plan to win the aunt's consent. Sneaking into the house again through an open window, he attaches a couple of sticks onto a pair of shoes behind a curtain, giving the illusion that a burglar has entered, and flees the scene. As the aunt and Mary discover the "burglar," they predictably panick and run out for help, whereupon Max conveniently appears at the door. He agrees to take care of the intruder with his bare hands, declining the offer of a gun. As he enters the room of the alleged burglar alone, our hero stages one helluva fight. At one point, Max runs about the room on all fours, carrying shoes both on his hands, as well as his feet; behind the curtain, of course, it looks as though the footwear on his hands belongs to the "intruder." Finally emerging from the room, seemingly wounded but alive and well, our brave gentleman is embraced by the aunt. As she disappears from sight, Max discreetly reveals the scheme to his bride-to-be and they share a good laugh.

For years after its initial release, this first reel remained the only available part of *Be My Wife*. However, given that the excerpt plays superbly on its own as a short comedy, it nonetheless found inclusion both in Maud Linder's 1963 compilation, *En compagnie de Max Linder*, as well as several DVD releases in the early 2000s. Finally, in 2012, the complete five-reeler was restored and brought back from oblivion, to the delight of Max's present-day fans. Considering the ingenuity of its first sequence, however, the rest of *Be My Wife* comes off as a bit of a disappointment, in this author's opinion. Max's violent confrontation with the imaginary burglar stands as one of the comedian's brightest moments. Like the "mirror routine," its basic premise may have been a well-used stage act, but Max's version appears to have popularized it onscreen (both Harold Lloyd, Charley Chase, and several others were to repeat the gag in subsequent years*). By contrast, the rest of the picture feels rather overlong, with little to offer in the way of story and character development, even less so than his previous effort.

* Harold Lloyd in *Dr. Jack* (1922); Charley Chase in *Mighty Like a Moose* (1926).

The eventual climax of the film should be suspenseful enough, as Max and his wife both believe each other to be unfaithful, but it's arguably less effective than it could have been, since we've been given no real opportunity to get to know these characters in the film's preceding reels. There are amusing individual bits and moments to be found throughout, of course. At one point, a mouse finds its way up Max's pants, forcing him to do "boogiewoogie" at his own wedding dance to ease the discomfort, but the scenes do not really merge into a satisfying unity. Again in this author's opinion, the foremost problem may have been that Max in this film relied on comic situations too much reminiscent of his work in France ten years prior, material that may very well have worked in that context, but not necessarily in a 1920s feature. Even so, as had been the case before in some of his other, arguably less remarkable, efforts, the gratifying presence of Max Linder still makes the five-reel version of *Be My Wife* worthy of repeated viewings.[181]

As always in a film book permeated with an author's personal opinions, it should of course be stressed that others may experience a given work differently. Indeed, by the time of *Be My Wife*'s official debut in Sacramento on November 6, 1921, the film had already pulled in some favorable reactions. One writer vouched that, while the film may not have been "as original" as Max's previous adventure, it had "enough laughs [in it] to satisfy anyone." Although some of the gags and situations were "not new" to the screen, Max nonetheless performed them "in a new way."[182] German critics also had good words to offer, making passing mention of his likeness to Chaplin "in the fundamental tone" of his humor, as well as "in many gestures."[183]

***Must-Get-There* Dart-In-Again**

Ever since he became his own director on a near-permanent basis in 1910-1911, Max had carried an authoritarian scent about him while on set. Although the comedian in later years tended to remember his years at Pathé with fondness, on occasion the constant demand for new farces had caused him—and his fellow performers—quite a bit of strain during Max's heyday. When a Spanish reporter later recalled to have "witnessed the shooting of a

Max Linder film" in France, the writer bluntly declared that even "Napoleon could not have given more strict orders [than Linder did] to his operators, stagehands, and other staff." Furthermore, "when something was not to his taste," his ensuing anger "was unleashed... against all. Thankfully," the writer joked, "the [silent] filmstrip did not contain his swearing."[184] If Max's mood swings could be challenging to others on occasion in the early 1910s, such difficulties likely became all the more striking by the 1920s. The mostly decent reviews of *Le petit café* and his first two American features notwithstanding, in candid moments, Max admitted that he did "not feel funny anymore."[185] Six years after his discharge from the army, he had not reclaimed the matchless spot he once enjoyed in the eyes of "movie patrons," and somehow, he must have known that he was unlikely to do so by this point.

Whether he felt like it or not, his comic mind still persisted. Having allowed himself a few weeks of deserved rest after *Be My Wife*'s release, by January 1922, he was already concocting his next feature, to be shot in Culver City. However, he quickly found himself bedridden once again, as his eyes were burned from a projector "designed to illuminate the décor of a... street." Thankfully, although doctors at first feared the worst, he managed to return to the film after a few days of rest.[186]

For his third American feature, Max decided on a (for him) rather unconventional concept. Given that Douglas Fairbanks' smash hit adventure, *The Three Musketeers* (1921), had been out for only a few months by the time Max began production on his own *The Three Must-Get-Theres*, there can be no question that the comedian indeed meant to lightly (or not-so-lightly) spoof Fairbanks' take on the well-known story. Moreover, in his performance as "Dart-In-Again," he actually seems to adopt many of Fairbanks' well-known screen mannerisms, his lovable nonchalance included.

At the same time, familiarity with Fairbanks' film is not required to appreciate Max's spoof. *The Three Must-Get-Theres* may just as well be viewed as a travesty on Alexandre Dumas' enduring 1844 novel. Following a preview screening in late May, where none other than Charlie Chaplin, Mary Pickford, and Douglas Fairbanks were present—apparently much enjoying the occasion[187]—the new five-reeler saw official release at New York's Strand Theatre on August 27, 1922, garnering a fair share of attention in the press. As Max had been persuaded to join the renowned United Artists* film company around the time of the film's making, it seems to have enjoyed a wider distribution than his two previous features.[188] While *The New York Times* claimed the film to be without "subtlety and pointed satire," all in all it was declared a "good-natured" parody providing "lots of fun." "The Fairbanks version runs along the line of the romantic," the writer noted, while Linder's travesty was found to run "along the lines of the ridiculous."[189]

Legendary critic Walter Kerr echoed this sentiment upon revisiting the film half a century later.[190] Although not necessarily an inaccurate observation, one could perhaps argue that, given the lightheartedness of the Fairbanks film it set out to caricature, Max was obliged to border on the bizarre to make his own film stand out, so amidst a scenario supposedly set in seventeenth century France, the film makes uninhibited use of such modern-day devices as motorcycles and the telegraph. In Europe, critics appeared more appreciative of such whims, a Swedish reviewer simply calling it a "[w]ell-done [film,] quick and sparkling with humor...."[191]

In hindsight, Max's presence once again assures the comedy its sense of real identity. Radiating less of Fairbanks' masculine appeal, perhaps, it's nonetheless striking how much Max's *boulevardier*—nearly unrecognizable in the film save for the grin and moustache—seems tailor-made for this part. One memorable (if quite macabre) gag has Max/Dart-In-Again being surrounded by an army of rapier-equipped men. As they point their razor-sharp tips against our hero, he gives us a sly smile and simply ducks, so that the furious soldiers wind up piercing each other instead. Incidentally, for his leading lady, Max this time hired Jobyna Ralston, who does a decent if rather anonymous portrayal of Constance Bonne-aux-Fieux.*

---

* United Artists had been famously established by Charlie Chaplin, Douglas Fairbanks Sr., Mary Pickford, and D. W. Griffith in 1919.

Although not among Max's subtler works, there is plenty enough energy and fast-paced creativity in *The Three Must-Get-Theres* to maintain one's interest throughout. Using Fairbanks' film (or, arguably, Dumas' novel) as its framework, it feels less episodic than his two previous features. Always the one to support a talented colleague, Fairbanks himself seemed not to mind the professional mockery. In fact, upon the film's release, the beloved superstar appears to have sent the comedian a telegram, stating *"Your movie is a great success in New York. Enthusiastic critics. Congratulations. Sincerely, Douglas Fairbanks."*[192]

Max was not in attendance at the film's première, however. Having days before become a member of United Artists, the comedian once more headed back for Europe on the *SS Paris* July 5. This excursion got off to a rough start, as he "arrived at the pier only to find that he had left his passport in the safe deposit vault of the Ritz-Carlton." As vividly recounted by the press: "He made a wild dash by automobile for the hotel while his secretary arranged with the Aeromarine Company by telephone to fly his employer to the [SS] Paris if Linder was left behind. Linder dashed back at the proverbial last minute, gave a fleeting kiss to two not unattractive girls waiting at the gangplank and started on his way [back] to France."[193] Reported by *The New York Times*, it at least makes for an entertaining story, if not an entirely believable one.

Idle yet again

As no new work materialized in the ensuing months, Max now saw no need to hide his lowered spirits to interviewers: "I have proof that [much of the public in America] has completely forgotten about me," he flatly stated. "Whenever someone called in my name . . . they replied[,] 'Max Lind'e? Who is Max Lind'e?' They do not know me [anymore]. Then they suddenly [will] have a bright moment. 'Oh yes, Max Lind'e, he's dead.' They thought I was dead[,] and I started to believe that I was deleted forever from the list of the living. . . ." On a brighter note, the interview did emphasize Chaplin's "great respect" for the comedian. Appar-

---

* Lovely Jobyna Ralston (1899-1967) was far from anonymous in her subsequent screen work, co-starring in six of Harold Lloyd's 1920s features, as well as dramatic vehicles such as *Wings* (1927).

ently, Chaplin had even tried to convince Max to stay in America, though to no avail.* Towards the conversation's end, the dejected comic made sure to laud the "extraordinary" works of Harold Lloyd, which he found to "surpass . . . everything one can imagine in the farce area."[194] (Lloyd, of course, at this stage had behind him such two-reel comedy gems as *Number, Please?* (1920) and *Never Weaken* (1921).

Other times, Max shared his thoughts on the European film market as it had now become, as opposed to the gargantuan industry of Hollywood: "In America there are studios three hundred meters long and seventy or eighty [meters] wide," he explained. There, "the studios are completely closed, without windows, as are used here [in Europe], to let the outer light get in. When you want to shoot, natural light will be out; for indoor scenes, [there] is spent a huge amount of electricity."

Perhaps surprisingly, Max also declared that France did "not have movie stars" anymore; "we have excellent artists from the theater that occasionally pose for [the] cinema," he said, but it was "not the same thing." The United States, on the other hand, could offer "numerous stars of both sexes."[195]

His argument that the era of European movie stars had entirely passed may be debatable, but from his perspective, it was a point well taken. By 1922, Pathé's once firm dominance on the American film market certainly belonged to a very distant past. However, although he did make plans to venture on a third trip, no more journeys to the land of the "numerous stars" would unfold for him. After six films divided over two occasions, the comedian had made his last American production.

Soon enough, other events were to take up his time.

---

* Indeed, Charlie Chaplin and Max Linder had gotten to know each other quite well during the latter's second stint in America. Footage of him visiting Chaplin's studio a second (?) time may be found in the documentary *Unknown Chaplin* (1983).

CHAPTER 18
MAX VAUNTS WITH GANCE

Max spent Christmas 1922 in the Swiss mountain of Rocher de Naye, a trip that resulted in more calamity for the comedian. French newspapers reported on December 26 that he had been victim of yet another serious accident,[196] which was elaborated in American press the following month:

"MAX LINDER FALLS 100 FEET IN ALPS CREVASSE AND HOVERS NEAR DEATH

"While on a farewell pleasure trip in the Swiss Alps prior to departing from Europe for Hollywood, where he has arranged to resume his picture-making activities, Max Linder . . . was overwhelmed by an avalanche of ice and snow which swept over a precipice into a crevasse one thousand feet below. Unconscious, he remained in this precarious position for several hours before his dog, which had escaped the onrush, attracted mountaineers by its barking.

"When, after great difficulty, Mr. Linder was rescued with the aid of ropes and he was removed to a hospital in Lausanne, the attending physicians thought at first the actor's neck was broken[,] but X-ray examination revealed the vertebrae as uninjured, although the muscles and tendons were dangerously twisted and caused the patient most excruciating pain . . . .

". . . both of the star's arms were fractured and he sustained serious internal injuries, the outcome of which is still in grave doubt."

The report adds that Max had planned to "arrive in Los Angeles about January 26 [1923] in order to get his next production under way by the middle of February." Now, his departure had to be postponed indefinitely, as it turned out. In the last paragraph of the article, it is claimed that his failure to appear in any new films in France since his arrival back home is due to "inadequate studio facilities and [some unspecified] unsettled political conditions."[197]

Rather than undertake a third American journey, Max decided on a prolonged vacation for himself, entering the popular ski resort of Chamonix-Mont-Blanc in mid-January. Despite his apparent conviction that he was all but "forgotten," the announcement of Max Linder's arrival at the mountain hotel is said to have caused quite a stir among the other guests.[198] While his intention may have been to enjoy a simple vacation as he recovered from his last accident, the stay in Chamonix would prompt big changes both to himself and to numerous others.

"The most extraordinary girl"

Sources cannot seem to agree on Ninette Peters' year of birth. The years 1906 and 1907 are often suggested, but by Maud Linder's account, Ninette was born on July 9, 1905,[199] incidentally four weeks to the day before the initial release of Max Linder's very first film, *La première sortie d'un collégien*. Her young mother, Mathilde Peters, had traveled from Brüssel to Paris three years before, partly to overcome a sad love story and partly in the hope of entering the Comédie Français as an actress.* Prior to Mathilde's departure from Belgium, apparently, a friend of her estranged father had suggested that she meet up with a male cousin of hers, who, in turn, introduced the young woman to an older acquaintance of his.[200] The name of the "acquaintance" in question seems not to have been publicly identified to this day. He was a man of considerable wealth, a "tycoon of the press and politics," who served both as senator and minister in his time.[201] (He is also said to have been a "rich Paris resturant owner."[202]) The two began an affair, and pregnancy resulted. Marriage was

---

* First founded in 1680, by 1902 the theater's present locales had just recently been renovated following a fire.

out of the question, but the stately man made sure to take good care of Mathilde and the baby financially, an arrangement that seems to have lasted until his death in the early 1920s.[203]

Thus it came to be that Ninette Peters grew up with her mother in Paris, essentially without a father, but in solid material comfort. (Note: although Ninette has also been attributed the names of Hélène, Jabe Helen, Jeanne, and Marguerite in various documents and press pieces, Maud quite consistently calls her by her pet name, "Ninette," in her two books, and she will be referred to as such here, as well.)

Upon their first haphazard encounter at the hotel in Chamonix, Max was entranced by the sight of seventeen-year old Ninette: "I spent the whole night in the hotel lounge talking to the most extraordinary girl I could ever imagine," he exclaimed to an architect friend. "Instantly I knew this to be the woman of my life."[204]

Despite one later report—possibly mere gossip—saying that Max had struggled at first to evoke Ninette's interest, as the girl was presumably crowded with "handsomer and richer" admirers at all times,[205] the two actually seem to have become infatuated with each other quite early. His health issues had begun to affect his appearance, for sure. Max looked decidedly older than his thirty-nine years in photographs of this period. Even so, he could still be a fun and charming companion when he put his mind to it. During his stint in Hollywood, he had proved to be an entertaining guest at social events, reportedly even engaging in practical jokes with Chaplin on occasion.[206] Young Ninette seemed to have found him quite delightful at first.

The newly-smitten comedian had not experienced his last accident of the year, however. While in Nice in early April, 1923, Swedish press reported that he had been victim of "a serious car accident . . . resulting in troubling head injuries."[207] The mishap was blamed, perhaps not too convincingly, on a mosquito in his eye, or, by another account, a fly.[208]

Be that as it may, barely two weeks later, he suddenly disappeared. The police were quickly notified by worried friends and relatives, and on April 29, the comedian found himself arrested on the grounds of "kidnapping" a minor.[209] The victim in question, of course, was Ninette, who seemed to have voluntarily run away from home with him. According to Maud, Max had planned for an escape to Monte-Carlo,[210] although newspapers of the day, including one Norwegian paper, claims the arrest to have occurred in "Nizza," or Nice.[211]

Mathilde Peters had expressed concern over her daughter's dalliance with Max, but did not want a public scandal and declined to press charges. Ironically, the incident still made it to the "scandal section" of the aforementioned Norwegian paper the following June, where it was announced that the comedian had "fallen in love with a sweet little niece of a senior government official* ... [w]ho was very willing to have her last name replaced with Linder's." The note reveals further, as Maud corroborates,[212] that the girl's "family said no, absolutely no; there should be no mésalliance with that comic." Although a single mother with a child born out of wedlock, at a time when such a thing was controversial, Mathilde's wealth had assured her a certain respectable social status that she wished not to tamper with. Max, however, seems to have taken "the situation with utmost ease. Long live publicity!"[213]

"Help!"—with Abel Gance

The allegedly "inadequate studio facilities" of Europe notwithstanding, by June 1923, Max was again back in business. Thirty-five-year-old director Abel Gance, even at that time notorious for his often lengthy productions, had agreed to direct the comedian in a two-reel comedy, apparently after Max bet him that he couldn't get a film done in three weeks.** (Some sources claim three days, which, in the absence of definite proof, seems unreasonable to this author. Clearly, Max had been persuaded to challenge Gance to do a three-week production precisely because such a schedule would seem unrealistic for a perfectionist like Gance, but not necessarily in and of itself.) Today celebrated for

---

*   It is not clear to the author if the "government official" mentioned here was, in fact, Ninette's stately father wrongly taken for her uncle, or if Ninette's father happened to have a brother who served as government official.

** At the time, Gance had recently completed his celebrated film, *La roue* (1923), running at 4 · hours. After his work with Max Linder, he embarked on his five-hour epic, *Napoleon* (1927).

his innovative use of lighting and editing, Gance was probably not perceived as an obvious collaborator with Max in the first place, and, indeed, the resulting film, *Au Secours!*, would stand out as an oddity in both men's respective filmographies.

Cast alongside actress Gina Palerme as his wife, Max here engages in a bet saying that he must stay in a "haunted castle" for an hour to midnight, or else pay up to the castle's quirky owner (Jean Toulout). A concept nearly done to death even by the mid-1920s, Gance's participation nonetheless makes this anything but standard silliness. Despite its customary storyline, the total combination of offbeat techniques in the film's "comic moments" gives it a genuine horror feel, more so than, say, Buster Keaton's *The Haunted House* (1921). Not only is Max bombarded with dangerous animals, giant skeletons, and lifelike statues while inside the eerie castle, he is also exposed to an abundance of spooky camera tricks, such as when his environment suddenly shifts to "negative" black and white. At one point, his appearance is duplicated three or four times, so that a small crowd of Maxes swirl about the room simultaneously. "African" masks pop up from nowhere, which, when coupled with the Noir-like lighting, evoke a truly scary effect. Amidst it all, however, gentleman Max still maintains his composure. Fearing that he will lose the bet, the castle's owner, who's watching from behind, cooks up an emergency scheme of sorts by hurrying down to the home of Max's sweetheart and appearing disguised as a monster outside her window as she goes to bed. Startled by the deadly sight, she desperately calls up to the castle where Max still resides, arousing supreme, sudden panic in our helpless hero. Those few minutes of his frenzied, tearful face covering the screen in close-up quite certainly represent the comedian's most emotional performance on film, even if one grants his early shots at screen drama prior to 1910. Brief though it is, the scene is genuinely alarming in its intensity.

Finally, of course, the ruthless "monster" reveals his true identity, and all's well again, though Max loses the bet, as he (technically speaking) does cry for help in the end. He is just relieved that his sweetheart is unharmed, and so all is forgiven.

The shooting of *Au Secours!* did not go without obstacles. In addition to certain technical problems—likely to be expected, the sizable use of "special effects" considered—leading lady Gina Palerme encountered difficulties as she prepared for her big scene towards the end. Bent on creating the right mood for the scene, the actress asked for the music of Saint-Säens' *Danse macabre* to be played during her performance, but instead, she had to make do with a section of Puccini's *Tosca*. Increasingly impatient, Gance yelled out his orders while Palerme screamed in a performance that, as historian Richard Abel points out, may not have been all acting.[214]

Released in early spring 1924, presumably in Prague on March 2, *Au Secours!* did not obtain the coverage that a Linder-Gance collaboration could be said to have deserved, if only for being such a sheer abnormality in and of itself. The author has not been able to find evidence that the film played a regular run in the United States. It did make it to several European countries, however, where Gance's name seems to have been downplayed in most of the film's promotion, as the public at large was no doubt thought to be more attracted by the return of Max Linder. Swedish paper ads announced the comedian's name in bold letters, proclaiming (rather deceitfully) the film to be an "exuberant, merry farce..."[215]

Meanwhile, in the very same papers surfaced reviews that were mixed at best. A Swedish critic found Max "rather faint compared to before. Some of the spooky antics are pretty funny," he admitted, "but a sparkling imagination for such material the two gentlemen [Linder and Gance] do not demonstrate..."[216]

Austrian press expressed similar objections: despite a promising start, it was said, "the ideas [after] are mournfully miserable and end up in a parade of... futuristic grim revelations without meaning and wit..." Max was applauded for doing "his utmost to disguise the humorlessness of his task," but "succeed[ed] only in part."[217]

Ultimately, *Au Secours!* probably plays a bit better today than upon its initial release. For one thing, especially if one regards the time in which it was made, it's tempting to look for parallels between the film's latter half and the works of certain experimental filmmakers of the era, the likes of Salvador Dalí and Luis Buñuel included. At least Gance's two-reel effort remains undeniably, visually intriguing to watch. As a comedy, however, it's arguably somewhat less successful. Because of its conventional plot and conclusion, and the instances of idiosyncratic camera trickery, it appears to be a film torn between two equally strong-willed identities. A divided identity need not be a drawback in a film, of course, but here viewers are left befuddled as to whether it's intentional or simply the inevitable outcome of a Linder-Gance get-together, with their respective backgrounds pervading the project in contrary directions. Even so, as one of Max's most atypical films, it's certainly interesting. Today, it also stands as his last readily available screen work.

Max may not have paid all that much attention to *Au Secours!*-s reception. More likely, other things were on his mind.

CHAPTER 19
MAX PIX CLICKS

On August 2, 1923, Max Linder married Ninette.* For such a celebrity of the early twentieth century, he had certainly taken his time to get hitched. In less than five months, he would be forty. While a Norwegian report told its readers that he had "tried to make his wedding as much of a sensation as possible,"[218] the couple seemed to decide on a rather discreet ceremony held at the Parisian church of St. Honoré d'Eylau.

As Ninette moved into Max's new high-class Paris apartment at 11 bis avenue Émile Deschanel,[219] the prospects for a happy union seemed tenable at first. Having given up on Hollywood, he nonetheless threw himself into new projects, penning a film scenario with the aid of his secretary. Although young Ninette, according to the secretary, seemed a bit frightened by her husband's sudden bursts of energy as he thought up new comic ideas, in the evenings they typically sat by themselves in the living room, holding hands and being obviously in love.[220]

Sadly, the family peace was soon put in jeapordy for both. Max, by several accounts, developed into a fiercely jealous partner.[221] He yelled out accusations of unfaithfulness at his wife and, eventually, even threatened to end her. Whenever he went to town alone in the evenings, it was said, he called her up to make sure that she had not gone out without his consent.[222] There seem to exist few accounts clarifying how, or to what degree, Ninette responded back.

Whatever the grounds for his jealousy, and there is reason to believe that most, if not all of it was based on outright paranoia, the manner in which he let his suspicions be known to his wife must qualify as severe mental abuse. While one cannot always be

---

* Although Maud cites the wedding date as August 23 (*Les Dieux Du Cinéma Muet— Max Linder*, p. 125), a notice unearthed by Renken suggests that it took place on August 2 (see *Nieuwe Rotterdamsche Courant*, August 4, 1923, or http://www.max-linder.de/chronicleE.htm#1923). A press piece in the Norwegian daily *Aftenposten* of August 18 seems to corroborate this, as well.

certain what is true or exaggerated in retrospective accounts of a given relationship, the eventual outcome of their union should put it beyond doubt that Max was a highly unstable companion by this point.

At the core of his fury and jealousy rumbled a grave case of depression. Friends from this period (for the most part unnamed) later recalled him to have had outbursts, such as: "I can't help it. . . . [i]f live I must, I feel it would be better if I had neither fame nor wealth nor love. If I were only a blind cripple begging pennies in the streets."[223] Perhaps or perhaps not an exact quote, but the message seems clear in any case. Although a lover of literature since way back, his tastes now appeared especially drawn toward the dark and macabre. He reportedly "knew by heart many of the morbid poems of Baudelaire," and also pored over Nietzsche's writings on voluntary death.[224] Apparently, he had also become a regular user of drugs such as opium by this time, which may have harrowed his mind even further, although no reports seem clear as to exactly when he began this habit.[225]

Towards year's end, Max undetook a short vacation with Ninette in Switzerland, likely hoping it would soothe their relationship.[226] The future looked brighter again; she was expecting a child. In Austria, a film crew eagerly awaited the comedian's arrival.

More drama—and another triumph

For the time being, at least, Max still maintained a lust for work. With a fresh scenario in his trunk, he arrived in Vienna shortly before Christmas, his wife again accompanying him, having made a deal with the Austrian Vita-Film company.* By one account, his contract assured him "£10,000" for forty days work,[227] or roughly $725,500 today.

After some initial uncertainty, French director Édouard-Émile Violet served as the film's director, while Max's scenario was to be followed more or less as planned. Austrian-born actress Vilma Bánky was chosen as leading lady.** Despite the lucrative con-

---

* Still in business, Vita-Film was first founded in 1919.
** Best-known for having played opposite Rudolph Valentino in *The Eagle* (1925) and *The Son of the Sheik* (1926), most of Bánky's screen work is sadly lost or unavailable today.

tract and a good amount of talent involved, the shooting proved precarious, to say the least. By now Max's mental state, possibly combined with opium use, seriously affected his ability to concentrate. He was said to have evoked "tantrum-like appearances at the studio."[228] Director Violet recalled that the fragile star seemed invariably "unstable, worried...."[229]

As winter neared its end, shooting had to be suddenly interrupted. On February 24, 1924, *The New York Times* stated in bold letters:

"LINDER WAS NEAR DEATH
"Film Actor and Wife Overcome by Sleeping Powder in Vienna

> "Max Linder... and his wife, who were found in a hotel room this morning in what was at first believed to be a dying condition from an overdose of sleeping powder, are rapidly recovering. The attending physicians reported that the serious symptoms which were apparent early in the day had disappeared, and they issued a statement... that the overdose was taken accidentally. The couple have been removed to a sanitorium."[230]

Despite the physicians' conclusion, which was taken "in accord with the judicial authorities who investigated the case," it seems evident in retrospect that the mutual overdose had not been accidental. In fact, even at the time, a few journalists dared to ponder on what the real motive for the near-fatal episode might have been.[231] Most likely, according to later accounts, Max had ordered his wife to take a high amount of barbiturates, whereupon he had swallowed a similar amount of the drug himself. However, it appeared that Ninette had only pretended to take her tablets, and then called for help as soon as Max went into a coma.[232]

Having recovered (at least outwardly speaking), shooting of Max's new film continued, wrapping up in April, after which he returned to France along with his pregnant wife.

Shortly thereafter, a first sneak preview of *Max, der Zirkuskönig* was held in Vienna, to the delight of its spectators. Eventually released as *Le roi du cirque* in France and *Circusmania* in English-speaking countries, the new five-reel feature found itself almost unaminously praised in the months ahead.* *Variety* freely declared it, after another preview showing in London, "without doubt one of the best comedies ever screened."[233]

The plot, as outlined by the journal, has Max playing a certain Count Max de Pompadour, whose dreamgirl happens to be a trapeze artist. Once again out of favor with his girl's father, our hero is told that marriage is out of the question lest he becomes a man of the circus himself (the role twist displayed here was doubtlessly intentional, because Max, with his ironic sense of humor, knew well that the typical predicament would have rather been to present a circus artist trying to impress someone of noble stature). Thus, he sets out to master various showman skills—acrobatics, flea-taming, and, finally, lion training—with mostly "disastrous results" until he ultimately "wins the day" through the help of a friendly clown. "[M]uch of the [comic] business is delightfully original," *Variety* continued, and "[m]oreover . . . never shows a trace of vulgarity" apart from a drunken act at the beginning.[234] A German critic liked the film well enough to suggest that it might "initiate a Max Linder Renaissance," having just before declared the comedian "an historical phenomenon."[235]

In France, reviewers were generally appreciative, as well. While one writer granted that the film's story may appear "banal" on the surface, "what cannot be told [in a summary] are the innumerable episodes and twists that come to graft on this simple idea[,] with a truly astonishing generosity and spontaneity."[236]

Despite later reports that the film did not go into general release until January 1925, it seems to have been screened in a good handful of European countries prior to the New Year. In Norway, for instance, it was put out before the public during the holidays of 1924.[237] On the other hand, as a foreign film it suffered a limited circulation on the American market.[238] Nonetheless,

---

* Although cited as a six-reel feature in *Variety*, it seems to have run at five reels in most countries, Sweden included (*Dagens Nyheter*, February 28, March 2, 4-8, 1925).

with *Max, der Zirkuskönig*, Max had made his most widely-lauded film in years. As his sixth feature-length effort—counting before it *Le duel de Max* (1913), *Le petit café* (1919), *Seven Years Bad Luck* (1921), *Be My Wife* (1921) and *The Three Must-Get-Theres* (1922)—a revival of this film is long overdue. The author has only been able to view an excerpt of it, obviously insufficient for an honest assessment, but its initial reception certainly suggests a very promising comedy. All personal troubles aside, somehow Max Linder still had it in him.

On June 27, 1924, still prior to the official release on *Max, der Zirkuskönig*, Ninette gave birth to a baby girl.[239] Although the child was to go by a variety of epithets before adulthood, she was initially given the name of Maud-Lydié. The event presumably brought a period of relative amity in the household, and Max seemed happy playing with the child.[240]

Following the success of his latest feature, the comedian was again considered hot property within the industry, at least as far as Europe was concerned. The first few months of 1925 resulted in a string of positive professional events.

In another press piece referred to by Renken, it was reported that the star had appeared on a Parisian radio broadcast in the evening of February 13, sharing anecdotes on his by now lengthy film career.[241] (Regrettably, as commercial radio broadcast was in its infancy at this point, there is next to no chance that any recording of this historical program was made, much less survives.) His comic creativity again in vigor, during the winter, he toiled with yet another film scenario entitled *Chevalier Barkas*. This next comedy was to be set in the late Middle Ages, with the comedian presumably playing a struggling knight. By May, a number of scenes had already been shot in the commune of Sion in southwestern France, where the production took advantage of "the most beautiful castles of the Loire."[242]

Also, as summer evolved, he was appointed new president of La Société des Auteurs de Films,[243] an organization founded, roughly speaking, to secure the various aspects of copyright to filmmakers.

While Ninette may have hoped—as he possibly did himself—that these encouraging prospects would lead to more stability at home, Max's frequent fits of rage still failed to cease. Finally, the terrified wife was thought to have fled, likely seeking shelter with her mother. After a month of separation, the couple reconciled, Max having "wooed [Ninette] all over again," as one account put it.[244]

By autumn, he had bought for them a new home, a lavish three-story brick mansion in the Paris suburb of Neuilly-sur-Seine. With the house furnished and servants hired, Max's upcoming feature, *Chevalier Barkas*, was well underway.

However, all of a sudden, he ordered all projects stopped. In the middle of October, he terminated his presidency at La Société des Auteurs de Films, and had his last will delivered, declaring that his daughter be raised by his mother, "a saintly woman," with his brother Maurice as "guardian."[245] He also sent his family a check of 3,000F, accompanied by a note saying, "In case anything should happen to me."[246]

CHAPTER 20
MAX DESCENDS TO AN END

On November 1, 1925, the British *Daily Express'* correspondent in Paris reported:

> **"MAX LINDER AND HIS WIFE COMMIT SUICIDE**
>
> "Max Linder, the leading French cinema star, and his twenty-year-old wife, Hélène ["Ninette"], committed suicide in the Hotel Baltimore, in the Avenue Kleber, here yesterday.
>
> "Both were discovered in a state of coma, and died without regaining consciousness, the woman at five in the afternoon, the husband twenty-five minutes after midnight [November 1]."

Ninette's mother had found the unconscious couple in their room: "[a]bout ten o'clock [AM] she [had gone] to the hotel where the couple had been staying for the past three weeks, but was told that her son-in-law had given strict instructions that he and his wife were not to be disturbed. The mother-in-law insisted, and finally the door of the bedroom was forced."

Max and Ninette had been lying "side by side on the twin beds . . . in their night attire." A "bloodstained razor blade" was also found. After a doctor was called, the still-breathing couple was sent to "a nursing home in the Rue Piccini [at 134 Avenue de Malakoff], where they were placed in adjacent rooms." The two "were found to have taken an abnormal dose of veronal and injections of morphia," whereupon "Linder had opened the arteries in his own and his wife's wrists before lying down to die."[247]

In hindsight, there seem to be some inaccuracies in the *Daily Express*'s report. *Washington Post* noted, in a rather long article on Max that was published six weeks later, that Ninette's mother had, in fact, been also staying at the Hotel Baltimore at the time, and "became alarmed when she arose for the early breakfast . . .

and saw nothing of [her daughter] and Max." Still more confusing, the *Washington Post* reported that Max "[t]he night before the tragedy . . . had seemed in unusually good spirits," and that "[e]arly the next day he and his wife were to leave with their eighteen-months-old baby to pass a few weeks at a friend's house in the country."[248] (*Daily Express* states, however, that little Maud was "in Switzerland" at the time, which is consistent with Maud's own account in her autobiography; she claims that she was attended to by her nanny.)

Max had almost certainly planned the suicide for at least several weeks, given that his resigning from La Société des Auteurs de Films and the delivery of his last will had both occurred two to three weeks prior, but he may still have been uncertain if he really would go through with it until the last moment. We cannot know for sure.

Exactly what catalyst had pushed Max's depression into a state of such despair, mania, or even insanity, remains unclear to this day. Most likely there were several factors at work. By several accounts, he had suffered from bouts of depression for a large part, if not most of, his adult life. It has also been taken for granted, probably with justification, that his experiences in World War I had to have had an impact. The *Washington Post* pointed out that many soldiers had come home from the battlefields much more seriously injured than Max, but still managed to lead reasonably successful lives afterward—which was true, but this point arguably undermines the various ways in which human beings react to severe stress. Max had likely been as unprepared for the horror of war as the majority of young men who had enlisted, and his depression history may have made the tension all the more pronounced. His friends also argued, reportedly, that he had been exposed to poison gas during his service, which if true may have wounded his mental health further,[249] but I have been unable to verify that. It seems unlikely, because only tear gas was used on battlefields during Max's time of service.

Through the years, it has also been assumed that Max's relative failure to recapture his worldwide fame after the war probably disappointed him, as well. The *Washington Post* cites more friends who claimed that he, in later years, had greatly tired of being a "funny-man," although he experienced at least some amount of success with his postwar output, especially with *der Zirkuskönig*. It seems perhaps doubtful that more recognition would have made a significant difference to him in the end.

Could Max's behavior in his final years actually imply clinical insanity? In the absence of definite proof, the question should probably remain open, but it does not seem far-fetched to this author to conclude that he likely suffered from serious paranoia or psychotic tendencies. His extreme level of jealousy toward his wife, which seems to have triggered his illness all the more, may have been a symptom of this. As there exists no known evidence that he was ever in a long-term relationship before his late marriage, one cannot say for certain either way if he might have proven himself a better husband at an earlier point in life. At this late date, it's impossible to estimate to what degree his opium abuse may have affected his conduct, as well.

In their own coverage of the tragedy, *Le Figaro* claimed that Max had left "six suicide letters," two to his parents, and others to his brother, Maurice, his secretary, his lawyer, "M. Durand-Villette," and his friend and fencer, Armand Massard.[250] Eventually, some alleged fragments from these letters were unveiled to readers, and if to be believed, these last writings appear to confirm that Max was in a volatile state of mind in his last days, for sure. For one thing, he accuses Ninette of having talked *him* into a death pact, which seems extremely unlikely. He also describes his wife as a "monster in the form of an angel." Unlike his parents, however, his friend, Armand Massard, had no faith in Max's allegations, and was instead convinced that he finally became "mad."[251]

Whatever conclusion one may reach as far as his sanity is concerned, there can be no argument that in the last two years of his life, if not before, he must have been a very unhappy man. That he was also, beyond all reasonable doubt, directly responsible for his young wife's death may make it harder for many to sympathize with his situation, which is understandable. In any event, one wishes that their lives had not ended thus.

In order to give permission for burial of the deceased, the "Magistrate in charge of the inquiry" needed to cite "suicide pact" as the official reason to the tragedy.²⁵²

Less than a week later, Hélène "Ninette" Peters was buried at a Paris cemetery with her mother present. Max's remains were brought back to his birthplace, where a ceremony was held at the St. Loubés Cimetière, his siblings following his coffin. On his headstone reads: *Notre Fils Regrette. Max LEUVIELLE dit Max LINDER De Cede. Le 1er Novembre 1925. A Lage de 42 Ans.*²⁵³

The value of Max's French estate, although not disclosed, was "said to be large." Indeed, his smaller "New York estate" alone was valued at "between $35,000 to $40,000" (equivalent to well over $500,000 today), not including the rights to his three American features, which comprised $8,000. In addition, there was "deposited in the Guarantee Trust Company more than $26,287.52."

To his friend, Armand Massard, Max left "a bronze by [sculptor Auguste] Rodin, his seats at the Ciné Max Linder, and his seat at the Théâtre des Noveautes." La Société des Auteurs de Films was bequeathed "10,000F." Cinematographic Press received "5,000F," while his chauffeur was "remembered with 2,500F."

However, "the bulk of his estate" was to go to his daughter, "Maud Lydié Marcelle Leuvielle."²⁵⁴

Max's last planned comedy, *Chevalier Barkas*, never saw release. In a morbid twist of irony, on the very same day as his sudden passing made headlines across the globe, a Swedish paper innocently announced upcoming screenings of the comedian's final completed film, *der Zirkuskönig*, which in Sweden carried the title *Max har Flax*, or "Max Has Luck."²⁵⁵

CHAPTER 21
MAX'S INTESTACY LEGACY

In the afternoon of October 31, as doctors had fought to keep the unconscious but still breathing Max alive, Jean and Suzanne Leuvielle received a telegram from a horrified Mathilde Peters, informing them that her daughter had died and that Max was in very bad shape. In her despair, she suggested that they meet.

Max's parents raced from their home in Bordeaux to Paris but did not get to see their son before his passing after midnight. Shortly thereafter, they made it clear that they did not wish to meet up with Mathilde Peters.[256]

As unreasonable as it may sound to outsiders, Max's parents were convinced that Ninette was directly to blame for their son's fate, and that *she* was responsible for the "suicide pact," despite so many testimonies stating that Max was the one who brought her into this. Whether the parents' conviction was genuine, or rather a strategy they adopted to suppress any ingrained feelings of guilt, it sparked a contempt for the deceased Ninette and her family that was to seriously affect the well-being of their grandchild, Maud, in the years to come.

Little Maud-Lydié now found herself, at sixteen months of age, literally deprived of both her parents. Despite Max's stated wish that the child be raised by his family, the grieving Mathilde Peters refused to let go of her grandchild. Aided by Maud's nanny, she eloped with the child to Colwyn Bay, Wales, where they went into hiding for months. Finally French authorities managed to track them down, delivering Maud to the Leuvielles at last,[257] and so the first of several vicious court battles ensued. Shortly before Christmas 1927, a Norwegian paper blasted:

"The Battle For Max Linder's Daughter"

"When film actor Max Linder and his wife died in Paris two years ago, they left behind a small daughter, who is now the central figure in a Parisian sensation process.

> "The parents of both spouses fight for the right to raise the little girl . . . the leading lawyers of France have taken on the case for the two parties.
>
> "France's previous prime minister [Alexandre] Millerand represents Mrs. [Ninette] Linder's parent . . . while the French socialist leader [Joseph] Paul-Boncourt [sic] shall protect the name and memory of Max Linder.
>
> "Over the [deceased] Linder-couple rests a secretive veil which has yet to be uncovered."

The article briefly outlines the couple's first encounter, adding that Ninette Peters by the Leuvielles' account had been a "corrupted" individual, while she, according to her mother, was repeatedly threatened with murder by her husband before their death:

"This lengthy agonizing tale is disclosed through a number of forthright letters, declarations and testaments, which the two lawyers submit [to the court], predictably in the presence of a packed and sensation-starved auditorium."

Midway through the report lessens in credibility somewhat, as the writer claims that the Linders had been killed by shotgun, an error sporadically repeated in the press throughout the 1920s. However, the last paragraph feels perceptive enough:

> "A journal [present] casually asked if it may not have been better both to the memory of the [deceased] and the child's future if the parties could come to an agreement in silence. However, the affair has now become a hot topic of conversation throughout Paris and splendid stuff for the boulevard journals, whose columns day after day wade in tales [on the case]."[258]

As noted in American press, during the trials, Mathilde Peters came "forward with a testimony showing that her daughter willed that the baby should be given to [Mathilde's] custody and 'on no account be permitted to be in the hands of [Max] Linder's family.'"²⁵⁹ As she had lived "in constant fear of being slain" by Max before her death, Ninette had been persuaded to compose a will of her own.²⁶⁰ This, however, seems to have been given little to no consideration in court.

A week later, another paper briefly noted that the case had been "settled: his brother [Maurice] got to keep the child."²⁶¹ The court held that "the right to choose a guardian rests with the surviving parent," who, in this case, was technically the husband, since Max had passed a few hours after his wife.²⁶² In practice, this meant that Maud was to remain with Max's parents, likely in part due to Maurice's then unidentified illness (later revealed to be syphilis).²⁶³

Yet, the bereaved grandmother would not back down. Informed by her lawyer that Max's will would be invalid if he could be proven insane at the time of its writing, the battle still roared throughout the winter.²⁶⁴ As the court found Mathilde unable to prove her allegations of Max's insanity, she had to declare defeat after all . . . for the time being.

Thankfully, Maud's beloved nanny, simply called "My Dear," was given permission to stay at the Leuvielle mansion, and Mathilde at least got to see the child during vacations. Yet, it was far from an ideal situation for Maud, who found the Leuvielles cold and distant, to say the least. In fact, she even recalled to not have been recognized as one of the family. As she grew up, then, she had good reason to believe that her paternal grandparents had been primarily concerned about the considerable fortune she was to inherit from her deceased father, more than her own welfare.²⁶⁵ The subject of her parents was a taboo in the house, so Maud grew up nearly unaware of what an illustrious figure her father had been in his time. For some reason, the Leuvielles were not even content with Maud's name, making her take on the name of Josette instead.²⁶⁶

As she approached school-age, curly-haired Maud longed for the vacations with her maternal grandmother, who, in her world, had become her "Maman," counting down the days for their next reunion. However, she'd usually be stranded with the Leuvielles for months at a time.

Finally, the case fired up again. In the spring of 1931, French press revealed:

"The Will of Max Linder
"Ms. Peters asks the court to declare it void

"It will be remembered that . . . Max Linder . . . died in mysterious circumstances . . . after the death of his wife on October 31, 1925. There was talk of crime, suicide . . . Then everything subsided.

"Max Linder left a will establishing his brother Maurice Leuvielle [as] tutor of his daughter Maud-Lydié Leuvielle.

"The Civil Court of the Seine, in a first judgment, entrusted the custody of the child to Mrs. and Mr. Leuvielle . . . The guardianship being left to M. Maurice . . .

"Here a new trial has just begun in front of the 1st chambre. This time it is an application for a declaration of invalidity of the will made by Ms. Peters, the mother of Mrs. [Ninette] Max Linder, under the pretext that the will . . . had been written a few moments before the death of the artist, and in a moment of dementia.

"Mr. Pierre Masse pleaded yesterday for the plaintiff, Ms. Peters. In a week's time, Maurice Leuvielle's reply will be heard."[267]

As the new battle lingered, it was emphasized in the press that Mathilde Peters this time brought "more than arguments" to the table. "She provided evidence. She filed a letter from a Swiss doctor who had noticed the madness of Max Linder [prior to his death]."

The Leuvielles' defender, again in the person of Paul-Boncour, declared the doctor's written testimony a "violation of professional secrecy," and asked the Court "not to take note of [the] letter." Although no one at the time could predict the eventual outcome of the case, the press report asserted that "the medical certificate in any case produced a strong impression. No one doubts ... the [alleged] madness of Max Linder [anymore]."²⁶⁸

Written testimony notwithstanding, by summer, Mathilde again left the Civil Court without victory:

> "Judgment was given ... against Mme. Peters, mother-in-law of ... Max Linder, in the case in which she demanded annulment of his will...."²⁶⁹

The case was up again in early 1935, with equally dismal results to Mathilde. By now, one can almost sense a trace of sympathy in the press toward both families. This, hopefully, would "put an end to the tragic adventure that defrayed the world ... and the couple who died ... can finally rest in peace," it was said.²⁷⁰

It seemed hopeless, to say the least, both to Maud and her "Maman." Then, all of a sudden, the tables were turned, and by autumn 1935, Mathilde finally received custody of her grandchild (by then eleven years old). The reason to the sudden shift, as Maud recalls, was as follows: as Maurice Leuvielle had refused to inform of his guardianship accounts, a commission was appointed to investigate the case, finding that Maurice was in fact squandering his late brother's fortune, and generally proved to be an unsuitable "guardian" to his niece. "It was then," Maud writes, "that Mathilde Peters proposed to Maurice to desist from the tutelage in her favor, against which, on her side, she renounced to pursue him and pledged to give him discharge of his management," to which he saw no option but to agree.²⁷¹

To young Maud, it was a day of relief, indeed, when she could finally breathe and escape the loathed mansion of the Leuvielles, with no fear of pursuit. In stark contrast to the court battles of preceding years, however, this consoling event appears to have received next to no coverage in the press.*

---

* The author recalls to have seen on the web a very brief notice of Maud and Mathilde's permanent reunion in a *New York Times* notice from 1935. However, I have been unable to find this notice again, despite efforts. From what I recall, it did not even mention Max Linder's name.

Unfortunately, Maud's joy was soon to wane, as Mathilde decided to send her girl to boarding school. From the child's perspective, this was abandonment all over again. Also, as Mathilde had finally become her official guardian, the grandmother turned out to be less cuddly, and their relationship grew strained as Maud reached adulthood. When the girl discovered, in her teens, that she was attracted to her own sex, she received no support from Mathilde whatsoever.[272]

She was brought up with only the vaguest sense of who her father had been. She eventually learned his name and that he had been a comic actor of sorts, but that was all. Even so, Maud became aware of Max's somber fate surprisingly early. At six years old, still too young to have grasped the restraint which the subject evoked in the house, she had casually asked her nanny what'd happened to her dad. No doubt a bit taken aback, the nanny decided on a straightforward route: he had ended his life when Maud was very small, she said, adding that this had made the little girl all the stronger, to not have been dependent on a father in life. Maud recalls that, at least at the time, this last point filled her with a feeling of pride.[273]

No one thought of exposing Maud to her father's hundreds and hundreds of films, for sure. To the contrary, the Leuvielles rather seemed to fight against such an occurrence, Maurice having reportedly wound up burning his brother's immense library of his own pictures, most of which had once been stored in a private vault.[274]

Yet, they may have known that, no matter how much they strove to curb Max Linder's legacy within the family, his artistic achievements could not be shattered altogether.

CHAPTER 22
MAX ENSHRINED IN TIME

Throughout the 1930s and 1940s, even as the surviving negatives of Max's films crumbled and his name stirred less and less recognition with the public, an occasional film of his still turned up at neighborhood theaters in Europe. Even after the coming of sound films in the late 1920s, sporadic silent revivals were appreciated among niché audiences. By her teens, Maud had developed a love of the arts and literature, movies included, yet it was only by accident that she one day in 1944, at the age of twenty, walked past a small film club in Versailles, to be shaken by the sight of a large poster announcing *"MAX LINDER en Sept ans de malheur."* While she obviously had no way of discerning that this was her father's first American feature-length effort—1921's *Seven Years Bad Luck*—there could be no doubt it was a work of his. She noted the date of the screening and, with no small amount of anxiety, reappeared in due time a few days later. As she stepped inside the entry hall, she was asked to show her membership card. Not being a member of their organization, she had none, but after a moment's hesitation, she revealed her identity in a timid whisper; and quickly found herself admitted to a seat of honor in front row.[275]

Thus began an elaborate, decades-long screen reunion with her father, whom she detested for having abandoned her, but nonetheless had to recognize as a great artist. As she came of age, Maud finally inherited her father's bequest, including the house in Neuilly-sur-Seine, whose furnishings had mostly been sold by that time. An ambition to restore his legacy evolved. Shortly before the death of Suzanne Leuvielle in the 1950s, the aging grandparent finally came to regret the family's dismal treatment of her grandchild, and she let herself be interviewed, sharing unique anecdotes of her famous son's upbringing, which would be of great value to Maud years later.[276]

Gone era back again

As the Baby Boom generation flourished, silent comedy experienced somewhat of a renaissance in public consciousness. The sudden rediscovery of several of Buster Keaton's films, thought to be long gone, was instrumental in this regard, as were the lively compilations of Robert Youngson, taking off with 1957's *When Comedy Was King*. Possibly in part due to his European origin, the works of Max Linder were given less attention in these years, yet the oldest of moviegoers could still recall his antics. When a Norwegian paper, in 1951, asked their older readers to submit personal remembrances of the silent era, one contributor singled out a Max Linder short for having been the first time he realized that a mere "film" could have real "content and narrative"[277] (he couldn't recall the film's title, but his summary makes it clear it's *Max asthmatique* (1914).

Film historian Jack Spears stressed Max's influence on the medium in the 1960s, all the more so in his pivotal book, *Hollywood: The Golden Era* (A.S. Barnes, 1971). Yet the person most responsible for Max Linder's resurgence among silent film buffs, certainly, was Maud. In 1963, Maud had Max's three American features compiled into the 90-minute *En compagnie de Max Linder*, which proved no small feat indeed. While *Seven Years Bad Luck* remained more or less intact, only the first reel of *Be My Wife* was known to exist at the time, whereas *The Three Must-Get-Theres* could only be unearthed from a damaged 16mm print, as the original source print had been destroyed in a bombing in WWII.[278] Released in France in the autumn, Maud's first compilation of her father's films was to be screened at numerous art houses and festivals in the years ahead.

As if tracking down the lost films of her father wasn't a sufficiently strenuous task, through the years, Maud had to spend literally a fortune restoring the often damaged prints she managed to find.[279] She'd juggle this ambition alongside her own career as a journalist. The results of these efforts came most vividly to light in 1983, upon the 100th anniversary of her father's birth, with the release of her second 90-minute compilation, *L'homme au chapeau de soie*—or *The Man in the Silk Hat*. Accompanied by an enchanting musical score by composer Jean-Marie Sénia, this loving tribute bestowed a healthy portion of Max Linder's heyday upon a new generation of spectators, and to this day it probably remains the best single introduction of his brand of comedy to unfamiliar viewers.

By the early 1990s, as she approached seventy, Maud finally decided to investigate the more painful, personal aspects of her parents' dramatic lives, which she had thus far tried to avoid, leading to her autobiography and a stunning book of stills on her father in 1992 (both of which, as anyone will notice, have been of utmost value to this biography and filmography, as well).

Nowadays—and beyond

In 1995, thirty-seven Max Linder short films were shown on French and German TV, carefully restored, as part of the series, Les Films Max Linder. A few years later, a selection of films thankfully saw release on DVD. First out was Grapevine Video's Comedy of Max Linder, which offered 14 Pathé-shorts (of admittedly variable picture quality). In 2003 came Image/Laughsmith Entertainment's Laugh with Max Linder, produced under the supervision of David Shepard. This single-disc collection provided a beautiful 35mm print of Seven Years Bad Luck, synced with an orchestral score by Robert Israel, as well as four early Pathé-shorts. Few new releases on the home video market materialized for the next several years, until the French company, Editions Montparnasse, finished their 3-disc box set, Le Cinéma de Max Linder (2012), presenting 10 crystal-sharp Pathé-shorts, as well as Maud's two compilations. Two years later, Kino/Lobster released their Max Linder Collection, serving present-day fans with complete versions of Be My Wife and The Three Must-Get-Theres, as they had not been seen for nearly a century. Later in the year, Spanish director Elio Quiroga completed, with Maud's cooperation, his documentary, The Mystery of the King of the Kinema, which was screened at the Gijon International Film Festival.

In Paris, the lights of movie theater Max Linder Panorama, previously known as Ciné Max Linder, still glimmered at 24 Boulevard Poissonnière.

His historical moment has indisputably passed, and the name of Max Linder is no more on the lips of the world *en masse*. Yet, new fans of his work still emerge, and long-lost films continue to reappear. We still find ourselves oddly bewitched by The Man in the Silk Hat, as he dives over cities on a couple of skis, escapes a horde of cops with a whole bathtub on him, or skates in his evening attire. We may safely conclude that the appeal of Max Linder's grin transcends his own time, as well as that of ours.

FILMOGRAPHY

The painstaking filmography compiled by Mr. Georg Renken for his website www.maxlinder.de has been of invaluable help to the filmography below. His findings have served as my predominant resource by far. Mr. Henri Bousquet's *Catalogue Pathé des années 1896 à 1914* has also been very helpful for corroboration. I have also, when possible, tried to find foreign release dates for Max Linder films (mainly through the Norwegian National Library and the daily *Dagens Nyheter*) to see how well these correspond with the findings below, which they invariably do very well.

I only include films where Linder's appearance seems to be reasonably well documented.

Pathé FRÈRES
1905-1917, 1919

La première sortie d'un collégien (August 1905) Director: Louis Gasnier. Cast: Max Linder. Length: · reel.

Rencontre imprévue (August 1905) Director: unknown. Cast: Max Linder. Length: · reel.

Les étudiants de Paris (May 1906) Director: Harry Ray. Cast: Max Linder. Length: 1 reel.

Julot va dans le monde (May 1906) Director: unknown. Cast: Max Linder. Length: · reel.

La puce gênante (July 1906) Director: unknown. Cast: Max Linder. Length: · reel.

Le Pendu (December 1906) Director: Louis Gasnier. Cast: Max Linder. 1 reel.

Lèvres collées (January 1907) Director: unknown. Cast: Max Linder. Length: · reel.

Au music hall (January 1907) Director: unknown. Cast: Max Linder. Length: · reel.

L'empoisonneuse (February 1907) Director: unknown. Cast: Max Linder. Length: · reel.

Les débuts d'un patineur (March 1907) Director: Louis Gasnier. Cast: Max Linder. 1 reel.

Pour un collier (April 1907) Director: unknown. Cast: Max Linder. Length: · reel.

Chaussure trop étroite (April 1907) Director: unknown Cast: Max Linder. · reel.

Idée d'apache (April 1907) Director: Lucien Nonguet. Cast: Max Linder; André Deed. Length: · reel.

Ah! Quel malheur d'avoir un gendre (April 1907) Director: unknown Cast: Max Linder. Length: · reel.

Nourrice par nécessité (May 1907) Director: unknown Cast: Max Linder. Length: · reel.

Ruse de mari (May 1907) Director: unknown Cast: Max Linder. Length: · reel.

Madame a ses vapeurs (June 1907) Director: unknown Cast: Max Linder. Length: · reel.

La légende de Polichinelle (June 1907) Director: Albert Capellani. Cast: Max Linder. Length: 1 reel.

Les péripéties d'un amant (July 1907) Director: unknown Cast: Max Linder. Length: · reel.

Les débuts d'un aéronaute (July 1907) Director: Lucien Nonguet. Cast: Max Linder. Length: 1 reel.

Le domestique hypnotiseur (July 1907) Director: Lucien Nonguet. Cast: Max Linder. Length: 1 reel.

Pitou, bonne d'enfants (July 1907) Director: unknown. Cast: Max Linder. Length: · reel.

Un drame à Séville (August 1907) Director: unknown. Cast: Max Linder; Magda Simon. Length: 1 reel.

Les exploits d'un fou (November 1907) Director: unknown. Cast: Max Linder. Length: · reel.

L'armoire (November 1907) Director: unknown. Cast: Max Linder. Length: · reel.

Le mari de la doctoresse (November 1907) Director: unknown. Cast: Max Linder. Length: 1 reel.

Les plaisirs du soldat (December 1907) Director: unknown. Cast: Max Linder. Length: 1 reel.

Mon pantalon est décousu (January 1908) Director: unknown. Cast: Max Linder; Jacques Vandenne. Length: · reel.

Ma montre retarde (January 1908) Director: unknown. Cast: Max Linder. Length: · reel.

Le premier cigare d'un collégien (January 1908) Director: Louis Gasnier. Cast: Max Linder. Length: · reel.

L'obsession de l'équilibre (January 1908) Director: unknown Cast: Max Linder, Jacques Vandenne; ?André Deed. Length: 1 reel.

La suspension (February 1908) Director: unknown. Cast: Max Linder. Length: · reel.

La femme sandwich (February 1908) Director: unknown. Cast: Max Linder. Length: · reel.

Vive la vie de garcon (February 1908) Director: unknown. Cast: Max Linder. Length: 1 reel.

Les pérégrinations d'une puce (February 1908) Director: unknown. Cast: Max Linder. Length: · reel.

L'obsession de la belle-mère (March 1908) Director: unknown. Cast: Max Linder. Length: · reel.

Retour inattendu (March 1908) Director: unknown. Cast: Max Linder; René Gréhan. Length: · reel.

Pédicure par amour (April 1908) Director: Charles Decroix. Cast: Max Linder; André Deed. Length: 1 reel.

La maîtresse de piano (April 1908) Director: Charles Decroix. Cast: Max Linder; André Deed. Length: · reel.

Une veine du bossu (April 1908) Director: unknown. Cast: Max Linder. Length: · reel.

Mes voisins font danser (June 1908) Director: Louis Gasnier. Cast: Max Linder. Length: · reel.

Un fiancé trop occupé (June 1908) Director: unknown. Cast: Max Linder; Jacques Vandenne. Length: 1 reel.

L'oncle à l'héritage (June 1908) Director: unknown. Cast: Max Linder. Length: 1 reel.

On demande un gendre à léssai (July 1908) Director: unknown. Cast: Max Linder. Length: 1 reel.

Un tic nerveux contagieux (July 1908) Director: unknown. Cast: Max Linder. Length: · reel.

Un jeune homme timide (July 1908) Director: unknown. Cast: Max Linder. Length: · reel.

Deux grandes douleurs (July 1908) Director: unknown. Cast: Max Linder. Length: · reel.

Le coup de foudre (July 1908) Director: unknown. Cast: Max Linder. Length: 1 reel.

Création de la serpentine (August 1908) Director: Segundo de Chomòn. Cast: Max Linder. Length: 1 reel.

Un mari peu veinard (August 1908) Director: unknown. Cast: Max Linder. Length: 1 reel.

Le verteux jeune home (August 1908) Director: unknown. Cast: Max Linder; Jacques Vandenne. Length: 1 reel.

Consultation improvisée (October 1908) Director: unknown. Cast: Max Linder; André Deed. Length: · reel.

Les tribulations d'un neveu (November 1908) Director: unknown. Cast: Max Linder. Length: · reel.

Un bobo mal place (June 1909) Director: unknown. Cast: Max Linder Length: · reel.

Aimé par sa bonne (July 1909) Director: unknown. Cast: Max Linder. Length: 1 reel.

Le petit jeune home (August 1909) Director: Louis Gasnier. Cast: Max Linder. Length: 1 reel.

Amoureux de la femme à barbe (September 1909) Director: unknown. Cast: Max Linder. Length: · reel.

Une conquête (September 1909) Director: Charles Decroix. Cast: Max Linder; Jane Frémaux. Length: · reel.

Un mariage américain (September 1909) Director: Louis Gasnier. Cast: Max Linder. Length: 1 reel.

Les surprises de l'amour (October 1909) Director: unknown. Cast: Max Linder. Length: 1 reel.

Petite rosse (October 1909) Director: Camille de Malhorn. Cast: Max Linder; Arlette d'Umès. Length: 1 reel.

À qui mon cœur (October 1909) Director: unknown. Cast: Max Linder. Length: · reel.

Le voleur mondain (November 1909) Director: Louis Gasnier. Cast: Max Linder. Length: 1 reel.

Roméo se fait bandit (November 1909) Director: unknown. Cast: Max Linder. Length: 1 reel.

En bombe (November 1909) Director: Louis Gasnier. Cast: Max Linder. Length: 1 reel.

La vengeance du bottier (December 1909) Director: unknown. Cast: Max Linder; Jacques Vandenne; Marguerite Montavon. Length: 1 reel.

Le premier rendez-vous (December 1909) Director: unknown. Cast: Max Linder; Jacques Vandenne. Length: 1 reel.

Avant et après! (December 1909) Director: unknown. Cast: Max Linder; Marguerite Montavon; Léonie Richard. Length: · reel.

Les exploits du jeune Tartarin (December 1909) Director: unknown. Cast: Max Linder; Jacques Vandenne; Andrée Divonne. Length: · reel.

La timidité guérie par le serum (January 1910) Director: Louis Gasnier. Cast: Max Linder. Length: · reel.

Une bonne pour monsieur, un domestique pour madame (January 1910) Director: Lucien Nonguet. Cast: Max Linder. Length: 1 reel.

Jeune fille Romanesque (January 1910) Director: Louis Gasnier. Cast: Max Linder. Length: · reel.

Le pacte (February 1910) Director: unknown. Cast: Max Linder. Length: 1 reel.

Je voudrais un enfant (February 1910) Director: Louis Gasnier. Cast: Max Linder; Lucien Boyer. Length: 1 reel.

Soldat par amour (February 1910) Director: unknown. Cast: Max Linder. Length: · reel.

Le serment d'un Prince (March 1910) Director: unknown. Cast: Max Linder; Mlle. Bièvre. Length: 1 reel.

Mauvaise vue (March 1910) Director: unknown. Cast: Max Linder. Length: · reel.

Une ruse de mari (March 1910) Director: unknown. Cast: Max Linder; Jacques Vandenne. Length: · reel.

Une représentation au cinema (March 1910) Director: Louis Gasnier. Cast: Max Linder. Length: · reel.

L'ingénieux attentat (April 1910) Director: Louis Gasnier. Cast: Max Linder; André Urban. Length: · reel.

Tout est bien qui finit bien (April 1910) Director: Lucien Nonguet. Cast: Max Linder. Length: · reel.

Kyrelor bandit par amour (April 1910) Director: Louis Gasnier. Cast: Max Linder. Length: 1 reel.

Amour et fromage (April 1910) Director: unknown. Cast: Max Linder. Length: 1 reel.

Une épreuve difficile (May 1910) Director: Lucien Nonguet. Cast: Max Linder. Length: 1 reel.

Le duel de monsieur Myope (May 1910) Director: Louis Gasnier. Cast: Max Linder. Length: · reel.

Le revolver arrange tout (May 1910) Director: unknown. Cast: Max Linder. Length: 1 reel.

Max fait du ski (May 1910) Director: Louis Gasnier; Lucien Nonguet. Cast: Max Linder. Length: · reel.

Max est distrait (June 1910) Director: Max Linder. Cast: Max Linder. Length: 1 reel.

Les effets des pilules (July 1910) Director: unknown. Cast: Max Linder. Length: 1 reel.

Max se trompe d'étage (August 1910) Director: Lucien Nonguet. Cast: Max Linder. Length: · reel.

Trop aimée (September 1910) Director: Max Linder. Cast: Max Linder. Length: 1 reel.

Champion de boxe (September 1910) Director: Lucien Nonguet. Cast: Max Linder; René Gréhan. Length: 1 reel.

Mon chien rapporte (September 1910) Director: Max Linder. Cast: Max Linder. Length: · reel.

Un mariage au puzzle (September 1910) Director: Max Linder. Cast: Max Linder. Length: 1 reel.

Les débuts de Max au cinématographe (October 1910) Director: Max Linder; Louis Gasnier. Cast: Max Linder; Charles Pathé; Louis Gasnier. Length: 1 reel.

La flûte merveilleuse (October 1910) Director: Max Linder. Cast: Max Linder. Length: · reel.

Un cross-country original (October 1910) Director: Louis Gasnier. Cast: Max Linder; Amédée Rastrelli. Length: · reel.

Comment Max Linder fait le tour du monde (October 1910) Director: Max Linder. Cast: Max Linder. Length: 1 reel.

Quel est l'assassin (October 1910) Director: Max Linder. Cast: Max Linder. Length: 1 reel.

Max prend un bain (October 1910) Director: Lucien Nonguet. Cast: Max Linder. Length: 1 reel.

Le soulier trop petit (October 1910) Director: unknown. Cast: Max Linder. Length: · reel.

Max cherche une fiancée (November 1910) Director: Lucien Nonguet. Cast: Max Linder. Length: 1 reel.

Max hypnotisé (November 1910) Director: Lucien Nonguet. Cast: Max Linder. Length: · reel.

Max manque un riche marriage (December 1910) Director: Lucien Nonguet. Cast: Max Linder. Length: · reel.

Max ne se mariera pas (December 1910) Director: Lucien Nonguet. Cast: Max Linder. Length: · reel.

Max a trouvé une fiancée (February 1911) Director: Lucien Nonguet. Cast: Max Linder; Jacques Vandenne; Georges Guy. Length: 1 reel.

Max se marie (March 1911) Director: Lucien Nonguet. Cast: Max Linder. Jacques Vandenne; Paulette Lorsy. Length: · reel.

Max et sa belle-mère (April 1911) Director: Lucien Nonguet. Cast: Max Linder; Jacques Vandenne; Paulette Lorsy. Length: · reel.

Vosin, voisine (July 1911) Director: Max Linder. Cast: Max Linder; Paulette Lorsy; Charles Mosnier. Length: 1 reel.

Max Linder en convalescence (August 1911) Director: Max Linder. Cast: Max Linder; Jean Leuvielle; Suzanne Leuvielle; Marcelle Leuvielle. Length: 1 reel.

Max a un duel (September 1911) Director: Max Linder. Cast: Max Linder; Georges Coquet. Length: 1 reel.

Max, victime du quinquina (December 1911) Director: Max Linder. Cast: Max Linder; Gabrielle Lange; Georges Coquet; Maurice Delamare. Length: 1 reel.

Max et Jane veulent faire du théâtre (December 1911) Director: Max Linder; René Leprince. Cast: Max Linder; Jane Renouardt; Gabrielle Lange; Henri Collen. Length: 1 reel.

Max lance la mode (January 1912) Director: Max Linder; René Leprince. Cast: Max Linder; Eve Lavallière; Jane Renouardt. Length: 1 reel.

Max reprend sa liberté (January 1912) Director: Max Linder. Cast: Max Linder; Gabrielle Lange. Length: 1 reel.

Max et son chien Dick (February 1912) Director: Max Linder. Cast: Max Linder; Jane Renouardt; Henri Bosc. Length: 1 reel.

Amoureux de la teinturière (February 1912) Director: Max Linder. Cast: Max Linder; Jane Renouardt; Gabrielle Lange. Length: 1 reel.

Max Linder contre Nick Winter (March 1912) Director: Paul Garbagni. Cast: Max Linder; Georges Vinter; Jacques Vandenne. Length: 1 reel.

Max bandit par amour (April 1912) Director: Max Linder. Cast: Max Linder. Length: 1 reel.

Que peut-il avoir? (April 1912) Director: Max Linder. Cast: Max Linder; Paul Landrin; Paulette Lorsy; Charles Mosnier. Length: · reel.

Le succès de la prestidigitation (April 1912) Director: Max Linder. Cast: Max Linder; Georges Coquet; Joé Dawson; Gabrielle Lange; Charles Mosnier. Length: 1 reel.

L'âne jaloux (May 1912) Director: Max Linder. Cast: Max Linder; Paulette Lorsy; Joé Dawson. Length: 1 reel.

Une nuit agitée (May 1912) Director: Max Linder. Cast: Max Linder; Jane Renouardt. Length: · reel.

La malle au marriage (May 1912) Director: Max Linder. Cast: Max Linder; Suzy Depsy. Length: 1 reel.

Max cocher de fiacre (May 1912) Director: Max Linder. Cast: Max Linder; Georges Coquet; Charles de Rochefort; Gabrielle Lange; Jacques Vandenne. Length: 1 reel.

Oh! Les femmes (June 1912) Director: Max Linder. Cast: Max Linder; Suzy Depsy. Length: · reel.

Idylle à la ferme (June 1912) Director: Max Linder. Cast: Max Linder; Suzy Depsy. Length: 1 reel.

Un pari original (June 1912) Director: Max Linder. Cast: Max Linder; Paulette Lorsy. Length: · reel.

Peintre par amour (July 1912) Director: Max Linder. Cast: Max Linder; Stacia Napierkowska; Gabrielle Lange. Length: 1 reel.

La fuite de gaz (July 1912) Director: Max Linder. Cast: Max Linder; Frédéric Muffat; Léontine Massart. Length: 1 reel.

Le mal de mer (July 1912) Director: Max Linder. Cast: Max Linder; Charles Lorrain. Length: · reel.

Amour tenace (August 1912) Director: Max Linder. Cast: Max Linder; Louis Gauthier; Georges Gorby. Length: 2 reels.

La vengeance du domestique (August 1912) Director: Max Linder. Cast: Max Linder; Jacques Vandenne; Charles Mosnier. Length: 1 reel.

Voyage de noces (August 1912) Director: Max Linder. Cast: Max Linder; Jane Renouardt. Length: · reel.

Max boxeur par amour (August 1912) Director: Max Linder. Cast: Max Linder; Maurice Tourneur; Charles de Rochefort; Hope Hampton. Length: 1 reel.

Max émule de tartarin (August 1912) Director: Max Linder. Cast: Max Linder; Stacia Napierkowska. Length: 1 reel.

L'entente cordiale (September 1912) Director: Max Linder. Cast: Max Linder; Harry Fragson; Jane Renouardt; Eugène Rouzier-Dorcières. Length: 2 reels.

Mariage au telephone (September 1912) Director: Max Linder. Cast: Max Linder; Stacia Napierkowska. Length: 1 reel.

Max veut grandir (October 1912) Director: Max Linder. Cast: Max Linder; Stacia Napierkowska; Jane Renouardt. Length: 2 reels.

L'enlèvement en hydroaéroplane (October 1912) Director: Max Linder. Cast: Max Linder; Georges Coquet; Andrée Marly-Coquet. Length: 1 reel.

Petit roman (October 1912) Director: Max Linder. Cast: Max Linder; Simone Le Bargy. Length: 1 reel.

Jalousie (November 1912) Director: Max Linder. Cast: Max Linder; Jane Renouardt. Length: 1 reel.

La peur de l'eau (December 1912) Director: Max Linder. Cast: Max Linder; Mado Minty; Gabriel Moreau. Length: 2 reels.

Max et la statue (December 1912) Director: Max Linder. Cast: Max Linder. Length: 1 reel.

La rendez-vous (December 1912) Director: Max Linder. Cast: Max Linder; Jeanne Bérangère. Length: 1 reel.

Jockey par amour (January 1913) Director: Max Linder; René Leprince. Cast: Max Linder; Marthe Debienne. Length: 2 reels.

Max est charitable (March 1913) Director: Max Linder. Cast: Max Linder; Paulette Lorsy. Length: 1 reel.

Les débuts d'un yatchman (April 1913) Director: Max Linder; Louis Gasnier. Cast: Max Linder. Length: 2 reels.

Mariages imprévus (April 1913) Director: Max Linder. Cast: Max Linder; Gabrielle Lange. Length: 1 reel.

Max Linder pratique tous les sports (April 1913) Director: Max Linder. Cast: Max Linder; Charles de Rochefort; Gladys Maxhance; Gabriel Moreau. Length: 2 reels.

Rivalité (May 1913) Director: Max Linder. Cast: Max Linder. Length: 1 reel.

Max et les crêpes (May 1913) Director: Max Linder. Cast: Max Linder; Jane Renouardt. Length: 1 reel.

Max toreador (June 1913) Director: Max Linder. Cast: Max Linder; Stacia Napierkowska; Angelina Villar. Length: 2 reels.

Les vacances de Max (July 1913) Director: Max Linder. Cast: Max Linder; Lucy d'Orbel; Georges Gorby; Gaby Morlay. Length: 1 reel.

Max n'aime pas les chats (July 1913) Director: Max Linder. Cast: Max Linder. Length: 1 reel.

Le duel de Max (July 1913) Director: Max Linder. Cast: Max Linder; Pierre Palau; Jane Ixe; Louis Baron. Length: 5 reels.

Le billet doux (August 1913) Director: Max Linder. Cast: Max Linder. Length: 1 reel.

Le chapeau de Max (August 1913) Director: Max Linder. Cast: Max Linder; Jacques Vandenne. Length: 1 reel.

Max fait de la photo (September 1913) Director: Max Linder. Cast: Max Linder. Length: 1 reel.

Max virtuose (October 1913) Director: Max Linder. Cast: Max Linder; Charles de Rochefort. Length: 1 reel.

Max fait des conquêtes (October 1913) Director: Max Linder. Cast: Max Linder. Length: 1 reel.

Max sauveteur (November 1913) Director: Max Linder. Cast: Max Linder. Length: 1 reel.

Max collectionne les chaussures (November 1913) Director: Max Linder. Cast: Max Linder; Lilian Greuze. Length: 1 reel.

Max illusionniste (December 1913) Director: Max Linder. Cast: Max Linder; Cécile Guyon. Length: 1 reel.

L'anglais tel que Max le parle (December 1913) Director: Max Linder. Cast: Max Linder; Cécile Guyon; Louis Baron. Length: 1 reel.

N'embrassez pas votre bonne (December 1913) Director: Max Linder. Cast: Max Linder; Geneviève Chapelas. Length: 2 reels.

Max pedicure (January 1914) Director: Max Linder. Cast: Max Linder; Lilian Greuze; Georges Gorby. Length: 1 reel.

Max est décoré (February 1914) Director: Max Linder. Cast: Max Linder; Henri Collen. Length: 1 reel.

Max professeur de Tango (February 1914) Director: Max Linder. Cast: Max Linder; Henri Collen; Charles de Rochefort; Hilda May. Length: 1 reel.

Max, maître d'hôtel (March 1914) Director: Max Linder. Cast: Max Linder; Lilian Greuze; Charles de Rochefort. Length: 1 reel.

Mari jaloux (April 1914) Director: Max Linder; René Leprince. Cast: Max Linder; Henri Collen; Emile Pierre; Carbrey Boys; Hilda May. Length: 1 reel.

Max et la doctoresse (April 1914) Director: Max Linder. Cast: Max Linder. Length: 1 reel.

Le pendu (May 1914) Director: Max Linder. Cast: Max Linder; Jacques Vandenne. Length: 1 reel.

Max joue le drame (June 1914) Director: Max Linder. Cast: Max Linder; Rachel Fabris; Charles de Rochefort. Length: 1 reel.

Mariage force (June 1914) Director: Max Linder. Cast: Max Linder; Jacques Vandenne; Charles de Rochefort. Length: 2 reels.

Max à Monaco (July 1914) Director: Max Linder. Cast: Max Linder; Lilian Greuze. Length: 1 reel.

Max ashtmatique (August 1914) Director: Max Linder. Cast: Max Linder. Length: 1 reel.

Max et sa belle-mère (August 1914) Director: Max Linder. Cast: Max Linder; Pâquerette. Length: 2 reels.

Cuisiner par amour (October 1914) Director: Max Linder. Cast: Max Linder; Lilian Greuze; Jacques Vandenne. Length: 1 reel.

Max au couvent (November 1914) Director: Max Linder. Cast: Max Linder; Lilian Greuze; Louis Baron; Germaine Rysor. Length: 2 reels.

Très moutarde (December 1914) Director: unknown. Max Linder. Cast: Max Linder. Length: 2 reels.

Dick est un chien savant (December 1914) Director: Max Linder. Cast: Max Linder; Renée Baltha; Pierre Piérade. Length: 1 reel.

Coiffeur par amour (December 1914) Director: unknown. Max Linder. Cast: Max Linder; Charles de Rochefort. Length: 1 reel.

Le baromètre de la fidélité (January 1915) Director: Max Linder. Cast: Max Linder; Jane Marnac; Geneviève Chapelas. Length: 1 reel.

Le sosie (March 1915) Director: unknown. Max Linder. Cast: Max Linder; Lilian Greuze. Length: 3 reels.

Tulipe merveilleuse (March 1915) Director: unknown. Max Linder. Cast: Max Linder. Length: 1 reel.

Le hasard et l'amour (September 1915) Director: Max Linder. Cast: Max Linder; Lilian Greuze; Armand Numès. Length: 2 reels.

Deux août 1914 (April 1916) Director: Max Linder. Cast: Max Linder; Gaby Morlay. Length: 1 reel.

Max victime de la main qui étreint (November 1916) Director: Max Linder. Cast: Max Linder; Muriel Cowan. Length: 2 reels.

C'est pour les orphelins! (January 1917) Director: Louis Feuillade. Cast: Léa Piron; Maria Fromet; Renée Barthou; Gabrielle Robinne; Marcel Levesque;

---

* Charity film; Max Linder appears in final sequence.

Yvette Andreyor; René Poyen; Edouard Mathé; Renée Carl; Léon Bernard; Jean Toulout; Ellen Baxone; Léonce Perret; Valentine Petit; Charles Prince; Lucy Mareil; Riri Rouche; Simon Gregoire; Georges Monca; Bahier; Madeleine Grandjean; Emmy Lynn; Josette Andriot; Henry Roussel; Sarah Duhamel; Fernand Rivers; Paule Morly; Marcelle Raynes; Huguette Duflos; Raphael Duflos; Max Linder; Stacia Napierkowska. Length: 3 reels.

Max et l'espion (February 1917) Director: Max Linder. Cast: Max Linder. Length: 2 reels.

Max et le sac (February 1917) Director: Max Linder. Cast: Max Linder; Geneviève Chrysias. Length: 2 reels.

Max entre deux feux (May 1917) Director: Max Linder. Cast: Max Linder; Marcelle Leuvielle. Length: 2 reels.

Max, médecin malgré lui (September 1917) Director: Max Linder. Cast: Max Linder; Lilian Greuze. Length: 3 reels.

Max devrait porter des bretelles (November 1917) Director: Max Linder; René Leprince. Cast: Max Linder; Geneviève Chrysias. Length: 2 reels.

Le petit café (December 1919) Director: Raymond Bernard. Cast: Max Linder; Wanda Lyon; Flavienne Mérindol; Andrée Barelly; Jean Joffre; Henri Debain; Armand Bernard; Francis Halma; Major Heitner. Length: 6 reels.

ESSANAY
1917

Max Comes Across (February 1917) Director: Max Linder. Cast: Max Linder; Martha Mansfield; Ernest Maupin; Helen Ferguson; Mathilde "Mattie" Comont. Length: 2 reels.

Max Wants a Divorce (March 1917) Director: Max Linder. Cast: Max Linder; Martha Mansfield; Francine Larrimore; Mathilde "Mattie" Comont. Length: 2 reels.

Max in a Taxi (April 1917) Director: Max Linder. Cast: Max Linder; Martha Mansfield; Mathilde "Mattie" Comont; Francine Larrimore; Ernest Maupain. Length: 2 reels.

LATER FILMS
1921-1922, 1924

Seven Years Bad Luck (February 1921) Director and Producer: Max Linder. Cast: Max Linder; Alta Allen; Ralph McCullough; Betty Peterson; F.B. Crayne; Chance Ward; Hugh Saxon; Thelma Percy; C.E. Anderson; Lola Gonzales (uncredited); Harry Mann (uncredited). Length: 5 reels. Distributor: Robertson-Cole Distributing Corporation.

Be My Wife (November 1921) Director and Producer: Max Linder. Cast: Max Linder; Alta Allen; Caroline Rankin; Lincoln Stedman; Rose Dione; Charles McHugh; Viora Daniel; Arthur Clayton. Length: 5 reels. Distributor: Goldwyn Pictures.

The Three Must-Get-Theres (August 1922) Director and Producer: Max Linder. Cast: Max Linder; Bull Montana; Frank Cooke; Caroline Rankin; Jobyna Ralston; John J. Richardson; Charles Mezzetti; Clarence Wertz; Fred Cavens; Harry Mann; Jean de Limur. Length: 5 reels. Distributor: United Artists.

Au Secours! (March 1924) Director and Producer: Abel Gance. Cast: Max Linder; Jean Tulot; Gina Palerme. Length: 2 reels. Distributor: Comptoir Ciné-Location Gaumont.

Max, der Zirkuskönig (September 1924/January 1925) Director: Edouard Emile Violet. Scenario: Max Linder. Cast: Max Linder; Vilma Banky; Julius Szöreghi; Eugen Burg; Ernst Günther; Viktor Franz; Kurt Labatt; Hans Lackner; Ilona Karolewna. Length: 5 reels. Distributor: Vita-Film.

BIBLIOGRAPHY
BOOKS

Abel, Richard: *The Ciné Goes to Town – French Cinema 1896-1914* (University of California Press, 1994).

Abel, Richard: *Silent Film* (Athlone Press, 1999).

Balducci, Anthony: *Lloyd Hamilton – Poor Boy Comedian of Silent Cinema* (McFarland, 2009).

Bousquet, Henri: *Catalogue Pathé des années 1896 à 1914* (Bures-sur-Yvette, Editions Henri Bousquet, 1994-2004).

Chaplin, Charles: *My Autobiography* (Bodley Head, 1964).

Cotes, Peter & Niklaus, Thelma: *The Little Fellow; The Life and Work of Charles Spencer Chaplin* (Bodley Head, London, 1951).

Dassanowsky, Robert von: *Austrian Cinema – A History* (McFarland, 2007).

Ford, Charles: *Max Linder – Cinema D'aujourd'Hui #38* (Éditions Seghers, 1966).

Ford, Charles & Hammond, Robert: *Polish Film – A Twentieth Century History* (McFarland, 2005).

Golden, Eve: *Golden Images – 41 Essays on Silent Film Stars* (McFarland, 2000).

Hays, J.N.: *Epidemics and Pandemics – Their Impacts on Human History* (ABC-CLIO, 2005).

Hayes, Kevin J. (editor): *Charlie Chaplin Interviews* (University Press of Mississippi, 2005).

Kerr, Walter: *The Silent Clowns* (Alfred A. Knopf Inc., 1975).

Linder, Maud: *Les Dieux Du Cinéma Muet – Max Linder* (Éditions Atlas s.a., 1992).

Linder, Maud: *Max Linder était mon père* (Flammarion, 1992).

Magnus, Philip: *Kitchener – Portrait of an Imperialist* (Dutton, 1968).

Mitchell, Glenn: *The Chaplin Encyclopedia* (B.T. Batsford Ltd, 1997).

Mitchell, Glenn: *A-Z of Silent Film Comedy* (B.T. Batsford Ltd - London, 1998).

Stein, Lisa K.: *Syd Chaplin - A Biography* (McFarland & Company, 2010).

Wakeman, John: *World Film Directors, Volume 1* (The H.W. Wilson Company, 1987).

Walderkranz, Rune: *Filmens Historia - Del 1, Pionjärtiden 1880-1920* (P.A. Norstedt &

Söners Förlag, Stockholm 1985).

JOURNALS / NEWSPAPERS

Various issues of *Aftenposten, Arbeiderbladet, Avisen, The Barre Daily Times, The Bemidji Pioneer, Berliner Tageblatt, The Billboard, The Bioscope, Blanco y negro, Bunbury Herald, Camera, Camperdown Chronicle, Caras y Caretas, Le carnet de la semaine, The Century, El Ciné, Le cinéma et l'écho du cinéma réunis, Cinémamagazine, Cinematographic Review, Classic Images, The Comet, Comœdia, La Correspondencia de España, Dagens Nyheter, Daily Express, The Daily News, Daily Press, Der Deutsche Lichtbildtheater-Besitzer, Evening Times-Republican, Exhibitors Herald, Feuille d'avis du Valais, Le Figaro, Film Daily, The Film Index, Film-Kurier, Fredrikstad Tilskuer, Fremtiden, Le Gaulois, Harrison's Reports, Hebdo Film, Heraldo de Madrid, Impartial, L'Intransigeant, Le Journal du Dimanche, Kalgoorlie Miner, Kinematograph Weekly, Kinematographische Rundschau, L'aiel de Paris, The Lake Century Times, Libération, Los Angeles Herald, Los Angeles Times, Milwaukee Sentinel, Morgenposten, Morning Bulletin, Motion Picture Magazine, Motion Picture News, Moving Picture World, El mundo cinematográfico, El mundo grafico, Neues Wiener Journal, New York Clipper, The New York Dramatic Mirror, The New York Times, The Nickelodeon, Nieuwe Rotterdamsche Courant, The Optical Lantern, Para todos, Petit Journal, The Philadelphia Inquirer, Photoplay Magazine, Pictures and Picturegoer, Pittsburgh Press, La Presse, La Publiciad, Recueil de la Gazette des tribunaux: journal de jurisprudence et des débats judiciaires* (July 1931 (A34) - December 1931), *Romsdals Amtstidende, Le Sentinel, Smaalenes Social-Demokrat, Stavanger Aftenblad, St. Pedersburger Zeitung, Sunday Times, Süddeutsche Filmzeitung, The Topeka State Journal, The Utica Sunday Tribune, Utstillingsavisen, Variety* and *The Washington Post.*

WEBPAGES

http://www.aftenposten.no
http://www.bnf.fr
http://www.dn.se
http://www.elephind.com
http://www.filmographie.fondation-jeromeseydoux-pathe.com
http://www.findagrave.com
http://www.imdb.com
http://www.liberation.com
http://www.maxlinder.de
http://www.nb.no
http://www.nyt.com

CHAPTER NOTES

INTRODUCTION
1. Waldekranz, Rune: *Filmens Historia - Del 1* (P.A. Norstedt & Söners Förlag, Stockholm, 1985), p. 207.

CHAPTER 1
2. *Classic Images* No. 441 (March 2012), pp. 73-85.
3. Chandler, Clement F.: "Max Linder Comes Back!" (*Motion Picture Magazine*, February 1917)
4. Ibid.
5. See Hays, J.N.: *Epidemics and Pandemics - Their Impacts on Human History* (ABC-CLIO, 2005).
6. Linder, Maud: *Les Dieux Du Cinéma Muet - Max Linder* (Éditions Atlas s.a., 1992), p. 6.

CHAPTER 2
7. "Une autographe inédit de Max Linder" (*The Century*, November 18, 1925).
8. Linder, Maud: *Les Dieux Du Cinéma Muet - Max Linder* (Éditions Atlas s.a., 1992), p. 7.
9. *Pittsburgh Press*, August 30, 1914.
10. Ibid, p. 13.
11. Linder, Maud: *Max Linder était mon père* (Flammarion, 1992), p. 140.
12. Sheridan, Oscar M.: "Charlie Chaplin's Professor" (*Pictures and Picturegoer*, July 1923).
13. Linder, Maud: *Max Linder était mon père*, p. 146.
14. Ibid, p. 147.
15. Sheridan.
16. Renken, http://www.maxlinder.de/crimedaix.htm
17. Linder, Maud: *Les Dieux Du Cinéma Muet - Max Linder*, p. 9.
18. Mitchell, Glenn: *A-Z Of Silent Film Comedy* (B.T. Batsford Ltd - London, 1998), p. 153.
19. Renken, http://www.maxlinder.de/deuxorphelines.htm
20. Linder, Maud: *Les Dieux Du Cinéma Muet - Max Linder*, p. 23.

CHAPTER 3
21. See Abel, Richard: *The Ciné Goes to Town - French Cinema 1896-1914* (University of California Press, 1994), pp. 14-17.
22. Ibid.
23. Walderkranz, p. 162.
24. Sheridan.
25. Ford, Charles: *Max Linder - Cinema D'aujourd'Hui #38* (Éditions Seghers, 1966), p. 103.

26   *Cinémamagazine*, November 25, 1921.
27   See Bousquet, Henri: *Catalogue Pathé des années 1896 à 1914* (Bures-sur-Yvette, Editions Henri Bousquet, 1994-2004), or Renken, http://www.maxlinder.de/dixfemmespourunmari.htm.

CHAPTER 4

28   See *Le Journal du Dimanche*, April 8, 1906.
29   *Le Gaulois*, November 7, 1906.
30   *Variety*, February 9, 1907.

CHAPTER 5

31   The October 5, 1908 edition of Norwegian paper *Fredrikstad Tilskuer* announces the screening of *Boireau som Arkitektlærling* (*L'apprenti architecte*, 1908).
32   See, for instance, *Evening Times-Republican*, March 19, 1915; announcing a screening of *Foolshead Telegraph Errand Boy*.
33   *Utstillingsavisen*, September 26, 1914.
34   Renken, http://www.maxlinder.de/aumusikhall.htm
35   Stein, Lisa K.: *Syd Chaplin – A Biography* (McFarland & Company, 2010), p. 30.
36   Synopsis in *The Comet*, April 6, 1907.
37   Ford, Charles, p. 13.

CHAPTER 6

38   Walderkranz, p. 205.
39   Linder, Maud: *Les Dieux Du Cinéma Muet—Max Linder*, p. 22.
40   *The Optical Lantern*, April 1907.
41   *Daily Press*, March 1, 1908.
42   *Kinematograph Weekly*, July 25, 1907.
43   Ibid.
44   *Kinematograph Weekly*, August 15, 1907.
45   *Kinematograph Weekly*, October 3, 1907.
46   *The Utica Sunday Tribune*, December 1, 1907.

CHAPTER 7

47   *The Barre Daily Times*, December 16, 1909.
48   *Le Figaro*, April 25, 1908. (Note: "ranter" is the author's fumbling attempt to translate the French word "fêtard.")
49   Renken, http://www.maxlinder.de/obsessiondelabellemere.htm
50   *Comœdia*, March 4, 1908.
51   *Comœdia*, Sept. 18, 1908.
52   Renken, http://www.maxlinder.de/roi.htm

CHAPTER 8

53   *Comœdia*, November 7, 1925.
54   *Moving Picture World*, July 17, 1909.
55   *The New York Dramatic Mirror*, October 9, 1909.

56 *Aftenposten*, October 5, 1909.
57 *The Bemidji Pioneer*, May 4, 1910.
58 *The Bioscope*, October 4, 1909.
59 *The New York Dramatic Mirror*, June 4, 1910.
60 *The Bioscope*, January 13, 1910.
61 Ibid.

CHAPTER 9

62 *The New York Dramatic Mirror*, May 14, 1910.
63 *The Film Index*, July 16, 1910.
64 *Moving Picture World*, October 8, 1910.
65 *The Nickelodeon*, October 1, 1910.
66 *Variety*, October 1, 1910.
67 *New York Dramatic Mirror*, July 30, 1910.
68 Walderkranz, p. 208.
69 *The New York Dramatic Mirror*, June 25, 1913.
70 *Stavanger Aftenblad*, November 22, 1910.
71 *Der Deutsche Lichtbildtheater-Besitzer*, November 24, 1910.
72 Georg Renken, email correspondence with the author.
73 Bonnat, A.R.: "Hablando con Max Linder" (*La Correspondencia de España*, October 4, 1912).

CHAPTER 10

74 *The New York Dramatic Mirror*, March 15, 1911.
75 *The Billboard*, May 20, 1911.
76 Synopsis in *The Bioscope*, May 4, 1911.
77 *Camperdown Chronicle*, September 26, 1911.
78 *The New York Dramatic Mirror*, May 22, 1912.
79 Linder, Maud: *Les Dieux Du Cinéma Muet—Max Linder*, p. 48.
80 *Moving Picture World*, October 12, 1912.
81 *The New York Dramatic Mirror*, July 17, 1912.
82 Walderkranz, p. 208.
83 *Caras y Caretas*, April 12, 1913.

CHAPTER 11

84 *The New York Dramatic Mirror*, June 12, 1912.
85 *Cinematographic Review*, April 14, 1912.
86 *Kinematographische Rundschau*, August 11, 1912
87 Renken, http://www.maxlinder.de/chronicleE.htm#1912
88 *El mundo grafico*, September 25, 1912.
89 *El mundo cinematográfico*, October 10, 1912.
90 *El Cine*, September 28, 1912. Cited: Silent Film Archive, 2014.
91 Eubank, Victor: "The Funniest Man on the Screen" (*Motion Picture Magazine*, March 1915). Reprinted in Hayes, Kevin J. (editor): *Charlie Chaplin Interviews* (University Press of Mississippi, 2005).

92 *El Cine*, September 28, 1912. Cited: Silent Film Archive, 2014.
93 *La Publiciad*, September 29, 1912.
94 Bonnat.
95 Renken, http://www.maxlinder.de/chronicleE.htm#1912
96 Ibid.

CHAPTER 12

97 Bueno, Javier: "Una entrevista con Max Linder" (*Caras y Caretas*, April 12, 1913).
98 Renken, http://www.maxlinder.de/chronicleE.htm#1913
99 *The Bioscope*, May 22, 1913.
100 *Berliner Tageblatt*, May 4, 1913.
101 *Bunbury Herald*, March 19, 1914.
102 *Aftenposten*, May 21, 1932.
103 Linder, Maud: *Max Linder était mon père*, pp. 160-161.
104 Renken, www.maxlinder.de/dueldemax.htm
105 *Kalgoorlie Miner*, February 21, 1914.
106 *Sunday Times*, September 14, 1913.
107 Georg Renken, e-mail correspondence with author. See also *Neues Wiener Journal*, November 27, 1912.
108 Lloyd, Pester: "Max Linder in Nöten" (November 20, 1913). www.maxlinder.de/PL201113
109 Walderkranz, p. 209.
110 Abel, Richard: *Silent Film* (Athlone Press, 1999), p. 201.
111 Renken, http://www.maxlinder.de/chronicleE.htm#1913
112 Abel, Richard: *Silent Film*, Ibid.
113 Ibid.
114 *St. Pedersburger Zeitung*, January 1, 1914.
115 *Arbeiderbladet*, February 29, 1932. See also Ford, Charles and Hammond, Robert: *Polish Film – A Twentieth Century History* (McFarland, 2005), p. 17.

CHAPTER 13

116 *The Bioscope*, November 22, 1917.
117 *L'Intransigeant*, March 18, 1914.
118 *The New York Dramatic Mirror*, December 9, 1914.
119 *The Bioscope*, July 9, 1914.
120 *The New York Dramatic Mirror*, April 21, 1915.
121 Linder, Maud: *Les Dieux Du Cinéma Muet – Max Linder*, p. 81.
122 *Fremtiden*, September 25, 1914.
123 *Romsdals Amtstidende*, September 25, 1914.
124 *The Washington Post*, October 1, 1914.
125 *The New York Dramatic Mirror*, October 7, 1914.
126 *Aftenposten*, March 22, 1917.

127 *Heraldo de Madrid*, June 17, 1915.
128 *Pictures and Picturegoer*, November 20, 1915.
129 *The New York Dramatic Mirror*, August 4, 1915.

CHAPTER 14

130 *The Bioscope*, February 25, 1915.
131 *The Bioscope*, March 25, 1915.
132 See Bousquet, Henri: De Pathé brothers at Pathé Cinema (1915-1927), Bures-sur-Yvette, (Editions Henri Bousquet, 1994-2004), or Renken, http://www.maxlinder.de/tulipemerveilleuse.htm.

133 Renken, www.maxlinder.de/chronicleE.htm#1915
134 Linder, Maud: *Les Dieux Du Cinéma Muet—Max Linder*, p. 82.
135 Renken, www.maxlinder.de/hasardetlamour.htm
136 Renken, www.maxlinder.de/chronicleE.htm#1915
137 *Le carnet de la semaine*, February 27, 1916.
138 Renken, www.maxlinder.de/chronicleE.htm#1916
139 *Hebdo Film*, April 8, 1916.
140 Mitchell, p. 155.
141 Linder, Maud: *Les Dieux Du Cinéma Muet—Max Linder*, p. 82.
142 Ford, Charles, p. 44.
143 Mitchell, ibid.
144 *The Topeka State Journal*, December 23, 1916.
145 *Moving Picture World*, June 16, 1917.
146 See, for instance, *Aftenposten*, April 12.
147 *Variety*, February 9, 1917.
148 *Billboard*, February 17, 1917.
149 *Moving Picture World*, February 24, 1917.
150 Chandler, Clement F. (*Motion Picture Magazine*, February 1917).
151 *Variety*, March 23, 1917.
152 *Moving Picture World*, April 7, 1917.
153 *Aftenposten*, March 28, 1919.
154 *Moving Picture World*, March 24, 1917.
155 *Motion Picture News*, May 5, 1917.
156 *The Bioscope*, July 19, 1917.
157 *Moving Picture World*, May 5, 1917.
158 *Variety*, March 23, 1917.
159 Chaplin, Charles: *My Autobiography*, (Bodley Head, 1964), p. 173.
160 *Photoplay Magazine*, Januar 1925.
161 *New York Clipper*, April 25, 1917.
162 Cotes, Peter & Niklaus, Thelma: *The Little Fellow; The Life and Work of Charles Spencer Chaplin* (Bodley Head, London, 1951). Norwegian edition, Tiden Norsk Forlag 1953, p. 135.

163 Ford, Charles, p. 139. As far as this author can see, Ford does not note any source for the Chaplin-quote.

CHAPTER 15

164 *Morgenposten*, October 24, 1917.
165 *Avisen*, October 27, 1917.
166 *Motion Picture News*, March 23, 1918.
167 *Moving Picture World*, June 30, 1917.
168 *Le cinéma et l'écho du cinéma réunis*, August 24, 1917.
169 *Hebdo Film*, October 13, 1917.
170 Renken, http://www.maxlinder.de/chronicleE.htm#1918
171 Linder, Maud: *Les Dieux Du Cinéma Muet - Max Linder*, p. 83.

CHAPTER 16

172 See for instance Magnus, Philip: *Kitchener—Portrait of an Imperialist* (Dutton, 1968).
173 *Film Daily*, June 6, 1920.
174 *Film Daily*, June 6, 1920. (Exhibitor's note, separate from review in same issue cited in the previous paragraph.)
175 *Neue Freie Presse*, December 10, 1920.

CHAPTER 17

176 Linder, Maud: *Les Dieux Du Cinéma Muet—Max Linder*, p. 109. See also Ford, Charles, p. 56.
177 Linder, Maud, Ibid, p. 110.
178 *Los Angeles Herald*, July 19, 1920.
179 *Exhibitors Herald*, September 25, 1920.
180 *Harrison's Reports*, March 26, 1921.
181 Some of these sentiments are based on an online review of the film by the author, initially written in 2007 and expanded upon in 2014. http://www.imdb.com/title/tt0011948/reviews-3
182 *Film Daily*, June 12, 1921.
183 *Süddeutsche Filmzeitung*, May 16, 1924.
184 *Blanco y negro*, November 22, 1925.
185 Wakeman, John: *World Film Directors, Volume 1* (The H.W. Wilson Company, 1987), pp. 671-77.
186 Ford, Charles, p. 56.
187 *Los Angeles Times*, June 2, 1922.
188 Ford, Charles, p. 65.
189 *The New York Times*, August 28, 1922.
190 Kerr, Walter: *The Silent Clowns* (Alfred A. Knopf Inc., 1975), p. 58.
191 *Svenska Dagbladet*, quoted in *Dagens Nyheter*, August 18, 1923.
192 Linder, Maud: *Les Dieux Du Cinéma Muet—Max Linder*, p. 124.
193 *The New York Times*, July 6, 1922.
194 *L'Intransigeant*, August 10, 1922.

195 *Para todos*, October 7, 1922.

CHAPTER 18

196 *Le Sentinel*, December 26, 1922. Kindly provided by Georg Renken through e-mail to the author.
197 *Camera*, January 20, 1923.
198 Linder, Maud: *Les Dieux Du Cinéma Muet - Max Linder*, p. 124.
199 Linder, Maud: *Max Linder était mon père*, p. 73.
200 Linder, Maud: *Max Linder était mon père*, p. 70.
201 Ibid, p. 68.
202 *The New York Times*, November 2, 1925.
203 Linder, Maud: *Max Linder était mon père*, Ibid.
204 Linder, Maud: *Les Dieux Du Cinéma Muet—Max Linder*, p. 124.
205 *Pittsburgh Press*, January 3, 1926.
206 Mitchell, Glenn: *The Chaplin Encyclopedia* (B.T. Batsford Ltd, 1997), p. 177.
207 *Dagens Nyheter*, April 6, 1923.
208 *Impartial*, April 6, 1923.
209 *Arbeiderbladet*, June 16, 1923. See also Linder, Maud: *Les Dieux Du Cinéma Muet—Max Linder*, p. 125.
210 Linder, Maud: *Les Dieux Du Cinéma Muet—Max Linder*, p. 124.
211 *Arbeiderbladet*, June 16, 1923.
212 Linder, Maud: *Les Dieux Du Cinéma Muet—Max Linder*, p. 125.
213 *Arbeiderbladet*, June 16, 1923.
214 Abel, Richard: *Silent Film* (Athlone Press, 1999), p. 33.
215 *Dagens Nyheter*, October 25, 1924.
216 *Dagens Nyheter*, October 21, 1924.
217 *Neue Freue Presse*, May 2, 1924.

CHAPTER 19

218 *Aftenposten*, August 18, 1923.
219 *The Philadelphia Inquirer*, April 20, 1924.
220 Linder, Maud: *Les Dieux Du Cinéma Muet—Max Linder*, p. 131.
221 Linder, Maud: *Les Dieux Du Cinéma Muet—Max Linder*, p. 132. See also *The Cairns Post*, December 22, 1925, and *Milwaukee Journal Sentinel*, January 29, 1928.
222 Linder, Maud: *Les Dieux Du Cinéma Muet—Max Linder*, p. 131. See also *L'aiel de Paris*, May 23, 1931.
223 *The Washington Post*, December 13, 1925.
224 Ibid.
225 *Daily Express*, November 2, 1925, and *Milwaukee Journal Sentinel*, January 29, 1928.
226 Linder, Maud: *Les Dieux Du Cinéma Muet - Max Linder*, p. 131.
227 *Daily Express*, November 2, 1925.

228 Dassanowsky, Robert von: *Austrian Cinema—A History* (McFarland, 2007), p. 34.
229 Linder, Maud: *Les Dieux Du Cinéma Muet—Max Linder*, p. 132.
230 *The New York Times*, February 24, 1923.
231 *The Philadelphia Inquirer*, April 20, 1924.
232 Linder, Maud: *Les Dieux Du Cinéma Muet—Max Linder*, p. 132. See also Golden, Eve: *Golden Images—41 Essays on Silent Film Stars* (McFarland, 2000), p. 78.
233 *Variety*, June 25, 1924.
234 Ibid.
235 *Film-Kurier*, September 17, 1924.
236 *Petit Journal*, March 6, 1925.
237 *Arbeiderbladet*, December 24, 27, and 30, 1924.
238 Linder, Maud: *Les Dieux Du Cinéma Muet—Max Linder*, p. 132.
239 Ford, Charles, p. 71.
240 Linder, Maud: *Les Dieux Du Cinéma Muet—Max Linder*, p. 134.
241 *Comœdia*, February 16, 1925. See Renken, http://www.maxlinder.de/chronicleE.htm#1925
242 *Feuille d'avis du Valais*, June 23, 1925. See also *Motion Picture News*, May 9, 1925.
243 Ford, Charles, p. 73.
244 *Pittsburgh Press*, January 3, 1926.
245 *Morning Bulletin*, February 6, 1928. See also *Recueil de la Gazette des tribunaux: journal de jurisprudence et des débats judiciaires*, July 1931 (A34) December 1931, p. 108.
246 Linder, Maud: *Max Linder était mon père*, p. 61.

CHAPTER 20

247 *Daily Express*, November 1, 1925.
248 *The Washington Post*, December 13, 1925.
249 Balducci, Anthony: *Lloyd Hamilton - Poor Boy Comedian of Silent Cinema* (McFarland, 2009), p. 108.
250 *Le Figaro*, November 2, 1925.
251 *Morning Bulletin*, February 6, 1928.
252 *The New York Times*, November 2, 1925.
253 https://www.findagrave.com/cgi-bin/fg.cgi?page=pv&GRid=8085&PIpi=11655206
254 *The New York Times*, September 4, 1927.
255 *Dagens Nyheter*, November 1, 1925.

CHAPTER 21

256 Linder, Maud: *Max Linder était mon père*, p. 16.
257 Linder, Maud: *Max Linder était mon père*, p. 21. See also *Recueil de la Gazette des tribunaux: journal de jurisprudence et des débats judici-*

aires, July 1931 (A34)—December 1931, p. 106.
258 *Smaalenes Social-Demokrat*, December 8, 1927.
259 *The New York Times*, November 21, 1927.
260 *Milwaukee Sentinel*, January 29, 1928.
261 *Arbeiderbladet*, December 17, 1927.
262 *The New York Times*, January 20, 1935.
263 Linder, Maud: *Max Linder était mon père*, p. 23.
264 *Morning Bulletin*, February 6, 1928.
265 Linder, Maud: *Max Linder était mon pére*, p. 23
266 Ibid, p. 24.
267 *Comœdia*, April 24, 1931.
268 *L'aiel de Paris*, May 23, 1931.
269 *The Daily News*, July 10, 1931.
270 *Comœdia*, March 7, 1935.
271 Linder, Maud: *Max Linder était mon père*, p. 60.
272 Linder, Maud: *Max Linder était mon père*, pp. 63-66.
273 Ibid, pp. 36-37.
274 Ibid, pp. 128-132.

CHAPTER 22
275 Ibid, pp. 104-109.
276 Ibid, pp. 133-149.
277 *Arbeiderbladet*, March 3, 1951.
278 Frenchculture.org: Interview with Serge Bromberg & Delphine Selles, December 5, 2013. http://frenchculture.org/film-tv-and-new-media/interviews/we-are-all-mad-about-max-interview-serge-bromberg-lobster-films-and
279 Prolongeau, Hubert: "*Max Linder, mon grand fils de père*" raconté dans "'*Max Linder était mon père*'" (interview with Maud Linder), January 21, 1995. http://www.liberation.fr/medias/1995/01/21/max-linder-mon-grand-fils-de-pere-raconte-dans-max-linder-etait-mon-pere_119024

www.ingramcontent.com/pod-product-compliance
Lightning Source LLC
Chambersburg PA
CBHW051926160426
43198CB00012B/2060